One of the key reasons companies fail  choose to stay busy, working hard on instead of leaning in to the struggle a hard work to create what's next. This accessible insights will help leaders revel in the struggle necessary to stay relevant in disruptive times. This book is highly practical and incredibly timely for all of us as we navigate the struggles of modern life.

— Peter Sheahan
Group CEO, Karrikins Group

Too many people are chasing goals that are exactly the opposite of what will bring vitality and fulfillment. In this playful and science informed book, Adam details the problem and offers a wide range of solutions. I know that many people will improve their psychology by reading and re-reading these pages.

— Dr. Todd B. Kashdan
Professor of Psychology and Director of the Well-Being Laboratory at George Mason University and author of *The Upside of Your Dark Side*

Adam Fraser has always had a clever way with words and stories, and he writes like he talks and presents. In *Strive* Adam gives us permission to feel anger, frustration, sadness and disappointment, and even to fail; and yet be fulfilled, grateful and content. *Strive* is a reminder to us all that stepping out of our comfort zone every day is key to our growth as human beings. *Strive* is a masterpiece in recognising the value of vulnerability, struggle and ultimately triumph as a person and as a leader. Keep struggling, keep striving!

— Avril Henry
Author, Keynote Speaker, Leadership expert

During my military career I achieved a number of firsts for women in the Australian Defence Force. To do this I had to tolerate a great deal of struggle and discomfort. At the time I didn't enjoy any of those situations where I was stretched or pushed outside of my comfort zone because they were uncomfortable. Yet I was able to manage my emotions and shift my mindset from resistance to one that embraced the struggle and challenge as something that could ultimately increase my skill set and see me achieving things far more than I thought I was ever capable of. If we can adopt an attitude to say yes to new challenges and embrace the struggle of difficult tasks, we might be surprised by what we, and our team, can actually achieve. Dr Adam Fraser articulates this concept so well in his new book *Strive* which provides you tangible strategies to lead a more fulfilled and purposeful life.

— Major Matina Jewell (RTD)

When Dr Adam talks, we should listen! An expert on performance, Adam's new book *Strive* will help you navigate the struggle and discomfort that can wear even the most resilient entrepreneur down.

— Emma Isaacs
Founder and Global CEO, Business Chicks

DR ADAM FRASER

EMBRACING
THE GIFT
OF STRUGGLE

WILEY

First published in 2020 by John Wiley & Sons Australia, Ltd

42 McDougall St, Milton Qld 4064

Office also in Melbourne

Typeset in Abril Titling 11pt/15pt

© John Wiley & Sons Australia, Ltd 2020

The moral rights of the author have been asserted

ISBN: 978-0-730-33741-6

 A catalogue record for this book is available from the National Library of Australia

All rights reserved. Except as permitted under the Australian Copyright Act 1968 (for example, a fair dealing for the purposes of study, research, criticism or review), no part of this book may be reproduced, stored in a retrieval system, communicated or transmitted in any form or by any means without prior written permission. All inquiries should be made to the publisher at the address above.

Cover design: Luke Lucas

Strive model illustrations: Jessamy Gee

Printed in Singapore by Markono Print Media Pte Ltd

10 9 8 7 6 5 4 3 2 1

Disclaimer

The material in this publication is of the nature of general comment only, and does not represent professional advice. It is not intended to provide specific guidance for particular circumstances and it should not be relied on as the basis for any decision to take action or not take action on any matter which it covers. Readers should obtain professional advice where appropriate, before making any such decision. To the maximum extent permitted by law, the author and publisher disclaim all responsibility and liability to any person, arising directly or indirectly from any person taking or not taking action based on the information in this publication.

Contents

About the author

Dr Adam Fraser is a heavy metal loving, car racing, daughter raising, gym junkie, geek researcher. Up until now the greatest moment in his life is being front row at an Iron Maiden concert.

But seriously his first love is his family (they were in the room while we asked him this). He has a gorgeous wife who, lucky for him, decided to lower her standards, and two daughters who have him completely wrapped around their little fingers. His #1 goal in life is to learn how to plait their hair. (Correction—Goal 1a is to work out what a plait actually is.)

His second love is research. The process of proving or disproving common-held assumptions seriously rotates his crops (we agree he needs to get out more). Dr Adam looks at the business and personal development world and is concerned with how much education is based on hearsay, fallacy or is simply made up. Business and life have become more complex and sophisticated. The quality of our education needs to follow suit.

Dr Adam has a PhD in Biomedical Science and his company conducts cutting edge research with different universities all over the world, then disperses that information in a practical form through books, keynote presentations, workshops, training programs, online programs and customised consulting projects. In the last 8 years he has delivered more than 1200 presentations to over 300 000 people globally.

He likes research so much he even researched himself (we know, he is out of control). He is thought to be the only keynote presenter in the world to have the impact of their keynote measured in a university study. Drum Roll! It improved the addressed behaviour by 43 per cent.

Most of all he hopes his work and research brings you value and, more importantly, helps you to be a better version of yourself for your family, your community and the globe.

Acknowledgements

The biggest thanks goes to my wife Christine. You are not only amazing and the love of my life but also one of the wisest people I know. Thanks so much for running defence for me on the home front while I was writing this book. You took one for the team. I love you.

To my daughters Isabella and Alexis, you are the spark in my life. I love you more than I could ever begin to describe. Thanks for being my guinea pigs and letting me mess with your minds—in a good way.

Thanks to my family, Mum, Dad, Sam and Doris. Your support and love mean so much to me.

To my team, Monica, Isabel and Rosemary for working so hard and making the business what it is today. Mon you have been by my side for a lot of years, I couldn't wish for a better right-hand woman, your ideas, insights and wisdom make my world so much better. Isabel thanks for all you do for the business and for the family too, you are an amazing role model for the girls.

Big thanks goes to the team from Wiley, Lucy, Ingrid, Charlotte, Chris and Bronwyn. You have all been a class act. Sorry Lucy I am sure this book gave you an ulcer. It took a while but we got there.

Alina Taylor, I appreciate you getting me to look at this book through a different lens. You really made a difference.

John Molineux thanks for not only being a great research partner but also a great human. None of this would have been possible without your hard work and dedication.

Bob Willetts thanks for having the guts and passion to engage us to develop The Flourish Movement. It has been a pleasure to work with you and it is one of the most fulfilling things I have ever done. To all the school leaders who have done Flourish, I have so much respect for what you do and at the very least society should give you all a weekly parade in your honour.

A big thanks goes to my teammates, who are the other researchers and professional speakers who support and inspire me continually. Thanks goes to Keith Abrahams, Amanda Stephens, Avril Henry, Matina and Clent Jewel, Dan Gregory, Kieran Flanagan, Simon Brakespear, Tim Longhurst, David Lawson, Dom Thurbon, Emily Heath, Darren Hill, Jason Fox, Glenn Capelli, Colin James, Allan Parker, Michael Steger and Todd Kashdan.

To Jen Jackson, the coolest cat I know, thanks for the advice on the cover. You rock!

Speaking of covers thanks to Luke Lucas for the amazing font.

Thanks to a few people who really helped get my speaking career off the ground, I will never forget the difference you made. Deb Claxton, Marg Booth, Winsome Bernard, Doug Malouf, John Tilden, Peter Sheahan and Matt Church.

Finally, thanks to all the amazing people who contributed to our research and helped us understand how to strive. I am forever grateful.

Foreword

The past decade or so has been accompanied by the prominent rise in dystopian visions of a terrifying future. One notable example, *The Hunger Games* series, literally pits people against each other as sacrificial representatives of their communities in a battle to the death. Generation Z and the Millennials have grown up in a world where seemingly every desire is at their fingertips and entertainment of every form imaginable ceaselessly streams toward them. They spent their leisure time glued to screens blasting away at each other in virtual worlds or watching children like themselves fight for survival.

Aside from the fact that the world seems to have been too lazy to bother to name either of us, Gen X shares at least one other similarity with our Generation Z children, the juxtaposition of a new era of convenience and comfort dawning before us with an attraction to apocalyptic doomsday futures. I still remember how the microwave oven transformed each of us Gen X slackers into kitchen maestros. One of the leading products was a microwavable ice cream sundae—you would "pop it in the 'wave" and out would come a cool ice cream treat with warm, oozing fudge topping. Once you got past the microwave name, this scary-sounding convenience miracle delivered on its vow of keeping the hot, hot and the cool, cool. Cable

TV and minivans promised to either bring the world to us, or bring us to it in comfort and ease. For my Gen X peers, we counterbalanced this sweet vision with *War Games*, *Mad Max*, and Steven King's *The Stand*. On top of this, horror movies flourished, whether imaginary (*Friday the 13th, Halloween, Nightmare on Elm Street*, etc.) or real, such as the macabre bootleg only-on-VHS phenomenon, *Faces of Death*.

On the one hand, life in developed economies had never been better, but on the other hand, visions of how easily all that good life could be lost and how grisly the aftermath might be pervaded the cultural landscape. As they do now. In one of the endless series of movies about comic book heroes, a powerful purple space ogre (no, not Grimace, my Gen X friends) puts on a bedazzled glove and with a snap of his fingers wipes out half of the life in the universe. I don't know if he got half of the mosquitos, but he definitely got half of the superheroes. In this world of virtual reality, 3D movies, streaming entertainment, powerful communication tools you can use to send your friends silly selfies or badly lip-synced videos, the most popular pop culture entertainment has been a portrayal of a world in which we're snuffed out, eenie-meenie-miney-moe style.

I met Adam Fraser in 2013 while doing a lecture and workshop series in Australia. I laughed my ass off during his talk and had so many light bulbs of insight flashing that I thought I had been outed by the paparazzi as Halle Berry's secret lover. One of my favorite moments, and one that I know many people connect with, was a side-by-side photo comparison of new and old playgrounds. The rubber flooring and rounded slides of the new playground contrasted with the rickety metal girders, splintered wood, and jutting rusty nails of the playground I used to run around as a kid. In fact, I still have a nice chunk missing from my shin bone from where I tried (and failed) to jump off the top of one of those extinct metal geodesic domes that passed for entertainment back then.

As much as I could spin unending yarns of life 'back in my day', the point of this foreword is to reflect on a vital, pressing dynamic Adam Fraser has pinpointed in this book. Despite the fact that people spend billions on both imaginary convenience (oh, the convenience of 80 emails and 2000 Slack messages every hour!) and imaginary duress, we seem to treat our penchant for laziness and ease as a manifest human right, and our innate craving for a bit of struggle and strife as mere fun and games. Two-day shipping is real, escape rooms and theme park haunted houses are pretend.

I think we have this completely backwards! Real comfort and convenience do next to nothing for us as beings who seek to grow, learn, and flourish. Instead this path weakens us, seduces us into dependence on whole galaxies of apps, gadgets, consultants and assistants. Fake struggle and strife also do next to nothing for us other than perhaps give us an inflated sense of our ability to deal with real hassle and hardship. What we actually need in order to grow, learn, flourish and have lives that matter is *fake comfort and convenience* and *real struggle and strife*. Only through work, effort, meeting challenges and being tested in our real lives do we find new insights, exceed our present limitations and construct meaningful lives truly worth living.

Through personal anecdote, professional experience, and most importantly empirical research, Adam Fraser shows us the power in digging deep and embracing that the difficult jobs in life, the uncomfortable talks, the nerve-wracking performances, the edgy interventions, the tough to swallow bitter pills of changing unhealthy lifestyles. What is even more remarkable is how fun and enjoyable it is to read this book. It is maddeningly difficult to talk about how everyone needs to have more agony and suffering in their lives without sounding bossy, glum or boring. Adam avoids this trap. With a deft touch for enthusiasm, intriguing examples, hilarious analogies, and the bemusedly shocked demeanor that cracked me up the first time I ever saw him present, Adam Fraser lays a persuasive and inviting path to a world that is intentionally a bit more difficult and a bit more challenging, but much, much more fulfilling.

In a real world beset by massive real struggles and real threats, we each need to step up and take on the challenges before us, particularly those that we would not ordinarily choose ourselves. Upon each of us now is bestowed the gift and the challenge to work for a better us and a better world. Let's do as Adam Fraser says and Strive on!

Michael F. Steger, PhD
Director, Center for Meaning and Purpose
Colorado State University, USA

INTRODUCTION
Why you don't want all your dreams to come true

These days, most people across the world are focusing on the pursuit of comfort and the avoidance of struggle – in other words, getting things without having to go through the hard work. We just want to be happy. We just wanna feel good. We want to have everything handed to us on a silver platter. We want to work on our strengths, building only on what we're good at and ignoring what we suck at.

But here's the bad news: this attitude is having a devastating impact on our mental health and wellbeing. Human beings feel most alive when they are courageously striving to overcome challenge and struggle. We get our sense of self-esteem and self-worth from being in the trenches, being forced to exhibit courage and evolve so we can overcome that struggle. Falling into the trap of spending all our time chasing happiness and comfort is destroying our lives.

What have you gotten yourself into by buying this book?

Forget the slow tease, it's totally overrated. Let's do the reveal right up-front. So what is this book all about? For more than ten years, I have been working on performance and wellbeing projects with my brilliant and wonderful research partner from Deakin University, Dr John Molineux. Through this research, we discovered a finding that totally blew our minds, and made us rethink everything we thought we knew about performance and stress. You see how most research works is that you have some sort of hypothesis (an idea about how something works), you review what research has been done in the past in the area, and then you set up an experiment to add to the collective knowledge on that subject. Our finding did not follow that formula at all. We stumbled across a discovery and then spent years trying to make sense of it. Trust us to do it the hard way!

It all started with a particular project, where we asked participants to complete a ten-day diary study. A diary study is where people record what they are doing at specific points of the day. We use this method because it greatly increases the accuracy of the data through people recording things in real time rather than in retrospect. Specifically, we asked people to record the tasks they were doing, how they felt during that task and the impact of that task on them. And we asked them to do this so we could measure the level of flow in their day.

No doubt, you've heard of the concept of flow, first described by the prominent psychologist Mihaly Csikszentmihalyi. It is a state of complete immersion in a challenging task. In fact, during flow you are so immersed and lost in what you are doing that time seems to vanish. As the following table highlights, the state is defined as being made up of five distinct factors: high in challenge, high in skill required, a feeling of time distorting, high in enjoyment, and high in interest.

Characteristics of flow

Challenge	High
Skill required	High
Enjoyment	High
Interest	High
Time	Distorts

Classic examples of flow are artists working on a painting when suddenly they realise it is dark outside and the day is over, or a scientist doing an experiment where they get so engrossed in the activity they forget about a meeting they must attend. Perhaps you've experienced it when your hour-long slot for a presentation feels like five minutes. Flow has been extensively researched and has been shown to not only be a state of high performance but also one that promotes excellent wellbeing.

The finding in our research that blew our minds was that the activities that built people's skill, confidence and a sense of achievement the most were not high in all five factors of flow. The activities that really built their self-esteem and self-worth and gave them a feeling of pride showed the following factors:

- *High in challenge:* It was very difficult.

- *High in skill:* They had to bring their A game.

- *A feeling of time distorting*: Most commonly, time seemed to disappear.

- *Low in enjoyment:* The task wasn't fun and they did not experience happiness while performing it. In fact, it often had high levels of negative emotion.

- *Low in interest:* They would rather not be doing it, and given the choice they would not seek out this activity. It was not appealing to them.

The next table sums these findings up.

Characteristics of skill and confidence building	
Challenge	High
Skill required	High
Enjoyment	Low
Interest	Low
Time	Distorts

Hang on a minute. Activities with low enjoyment and low interest are actually good for us? WTF?! This was not supposed to be true. So I decided we should keep studying this finding in more and more groups—and we kept finding the same thing. When we interviewed our study participants they said things like, 'Yeah, flow is awesome and it feels great, but the tasks and activities that really build my skill and confidence are the scary stuff that afterwards I think, *How the hell did I pull that off?*'. Moreover, when the people in the study talked about these types of activities, they said that as they entered the activity they felt all sorts of negative emotions, such as fear, anxiety and panic. And they often had negative thoughts, such as predicting a disastrous outcome. Say they had to have a difficult conversation with a peer or direct report, for example. They dreaded having the conversation and often predicted that the conversation would go badly. Despite their negative thoughts and emotions, participants who chose to meet the difficult situation head on did so by focusing on four things:

1. the compelling reason for having the conversation (in other words, the meaning and purpose associated with it)

2. the courage they would show by completing the action

3. the development and growth they would gain

4. accepting that it was not going to feel good but that was okay.

While these moments were not enjoyable or fun, after they had completed them people reflected on them with a sense of awe. They were in awe of themselves for being capable of overcoming such a challenging situation. They told us, 'these are the moments that count'; these are the moments where they truly grew and evolved. One participant described them as the moments where they get in the trenches and fight it out with the things that scare them. These moments provide huge benefit as you crawl out of the trenches to find a new and better version of yourself, a version that has evolved and grown.

> **Striving equals taking on challenging activities that require us to be brave and evolve in the pursuit of something that is purposeful and important.**

I define this as the state of striving. Striving is where we tackle difficult things (high in challenge and requiring a high level of skill) and have to display courage (overcoming low enjoyment and low interest) in the pursuit of a meaningful goal, aspiration or vision. Striving equals taking on challenging activities that require us to be brave and evolve in the pursuit of something that is purposeful and important. It is a critical and necessary state that leads to huge levels of fulfilment and transformation. The sad reality is most people are not engaging in it nearly enough.

As you move through the book you will see the Strive model gradually unveiled. A new piece of the model will be revealed in each chapter to help you see where you are on the Strive journey. Cool hey!

My ultimate goal

In the following chapters, I cover the specifics of striving and why you should want to do it more often. I explain how to practically strive but, most of all, I convince you that in order to have a rich life you have to get in the trenches with things that scare you, fight it out and celebrate when you crawl out the other side.

If you are now thinking, *Shit! Why did I buy this book? I'm not interested in doing things that make me uncomfortable. I was more after a book that has five easy steps to high performance, or one that sorts out my life in 12 super simple strategies.* Well, let me tell you that easy sucks. In fact, let me prove it to you!

Picture 'paradise'. What does it look like?

I'm sure in your version of paradise you have plenty of money and nice things—of course, lots of nice things. Flash cars, expensive clothes, big—no, *offensively* big—houses, swimming pools, jewellery... hell, yes! A boatload of jewellery. Is something missing? Perhaps work? But you're scoffing, right? Work does not exist in most people's paradise or, if it does, it's work that has very little stress and low expectation. Sounds good, doesn't it? The stuff of dreams? Wanna go?

Counterintuitively, if you want to have a fulfilled life, if you want to have strong self-esteem and if you want to be the best version of yourself, you need to avoid this kind of 'paradise' like the plague. The reality is that the environment I have just described is not a healthy one. How do I know? Well, I have been to 'paradise' and it totally changed the way I viewed happiness and fulfilment. Because the paradise I went to is killing people's souls.

Paradise is a place on earth?

It all started with a simple phone call.

I was walking down George Street in Sydney when my mobile phone rang. I answered and was greeted by a woman with a very thick Arabic accent.

'My name is Intisar. I saw you present at the Dalai Lama happiness conference and we would like you to come to Kuwait and help us make the country happier.' My initial thought was, *Of course you do. I get these calls all the time.* I thought for certain this was a scam. (I later found out Intisar's representatives had sent us three emails and my team had deleted them all because they also thought it was some sort of hoax.)

The next thought my sceptical mind had was that my mates had paid this woman to prank call me. (They do hideously mean stuff like this all the time. They once hired an actor to convince me that

60 Minutes was going to do a story on my research. After hanging up the phone from the actor, who I thought was a reporter, I was so excited. I called my mum, I called my top clients, and then finally called my best friend and said, 'Dude, you would not believe the day I have had'—at which point, he burst out laughing. Anyway, I digress; I'm just trying to show you that they are awful.) Thinking that this was my mates' doing, I started being incredibly rude to this woman. I demanded payment in rubies. I said to her, 'I will need a camel'. As expected, she was shocked and questioned this request. But I stayed firm, insisting 'the camel is a deal-breaker; I must have a camel'.

I can't remember what she said, but have you ever had that moment where your body goes hot from head to toe with embarrassment? Because this was the moment I realised the phone call was real. The most mortifying part was that the woman who I was being increasingly rude to goes by the title of 'Sheikha', which means 'princess' in Kuwait. The Princess of Kuwait calls me to go work on this project? You can't make this stuff up.

Luckily, due to her amazing sense of humour, we got past this embarrassing introduction and over the next four years I travelled to Kuwait to work on making the country happier. The organisation driving this project is called Alnowair, a not-for-profit initiative founded by Sheikha Intisar, who is also the CEO. A true patriot, Intisar saw greater potential for Kuwait to evolve as a society; for the people to elevate their level of happiness and joy to match the amazing country in which they lived, that was rich in not only money but also opportunity, history and culture. So she set up Alnowair to make Kuwait a more positive and thriving society.

When I first met Intisar, I was struck by her presence. Her enthusiasm and laughter light up any room, beyond her beauty and her sea of thick black hair. Intisar has a zest and a liveliness that is rarely seen, and a laugh that is never forgotten. I've met a lot of successful people, but what stands out about her to me is her curiosity and constant striving to find what is next, or what she can do that people have recently said is impossible.

Getting to know the country of Kuwait has been a fascinating experience. The Kuwaitis are beautiful people and I've truly fallen in love with them and their country. As I write this I experience pings of sadness because I flat out miss them. I have fallen for their food (a mate of mine, Darren Hill, was on one of the trips and coined the phrase 'Wanna put on weight? Come to Kuwait!'), amazing history, and the ever-present feeling of safety. I miss so many things about being there, but in particular I miss the call to prayer, which fills me with a Zen-like state every time I hear it. It's hauntingly beautiful. I have even fallen in love with the complexity and beauty of the language, and the last time I was there I did the first couple of minutes of my presentation in Arabic.

Even though I love the country, something is missing. While the people were kind, smart, articulate and incredibly hospitable, something was not quite right. At first, I couldn't put my finger on what was wrong, other than to say there was a percentage of the population that didn't have the zest, passion and energy that I'd found in Intisar. They lacked fire. They existed but they didn't really live.

When did smiling become a problem?

So I did what any self-respecting researcher would do and turned to the literature. The research I looked at indicated that Kuwait's global happiness ratings were dropping. In fact, some reports showed that they had a (lack of) smiling problem, and people's levels of happiness and wellbeing did not match the amazing privilege and comfort that living in one of the world's richest countries afforded them.

Many people who had lived in Kuwait for a long period said that the number of privileged people who spent their time complaining about insignificant issues had increased. However, Kuwait was not always like this, and has a history of being incredibly resilient and overcoming insurmountable struggle. They had to learn how to live in an incredibly arid and harsh landscape, and then were nearly wiped out by plague. But in true Kuwait style they fought back and once again flourished. They became incredibly skilled at trading and grew into the trading hub of the Middle East. Due to changes in economic conditions and the global landscape, that prosperity was threatened, but then oil was discovered and financially the country has prospered ever since, even though they have suffered through war and the threat of invasion. To sum up Kuwait's history, its people have been regularly knocked to the ground but each time they have gotten up swinging and come out of it stronger.

So what has changed in modern-day Kuwait? Before I get into the detail we have to acknowledge that there are many factors to consider when making broad statements about what contributes to an entire country's happiness. One such factor is that the concept of focusing on happiness and being more positive has not been a cultural focus for the Kuwaitis. It is a relatively new idea. However our research uncovered a surprising aspect of their culture that is having a negative impact on their wellbeing. It's simply too easy to live there. To put it bluntly they have too much money. (Just pause to let that sink in.) In other words, the Kuwaitis don't have enough struggle and challenge.

Due to the above revelation you are probably now thinking everyone in Kuwait lives in a palace, has seven Ferraris and walks their lions on a gold leash. To be truthful there is that element. I have been for dinner at houses that had pools and grounds similar to those that you would find in a five-star resort. At one dinner on my last trip, a guest was an 18-year-old male who showed up in a brand-new Bentley. Being a car nut, I asked him if it was his parents' car. He said, 'Oh no it's mine!' And then proceeded to list the other cars he had: another Bentley, two Rolls-Royces and a Ferrari. He then discussed his significant watch collection. My not too subtle Australian companion asked what the one he was wearing was worth; a quarter of a million US dollars was the answer. Also, I did meet a guy with lions. After he showed me a picture of his pet lions I said, 'Dude how do you get lions?' He looked at me like I was stupid and said, 'Um, you buy a lion, that's how you get them!' However those experiences are not the norm, they only apply to a minority.

Having said that the citizens are not struggling. The level of wealth for the average Kuwaiti national is high. One of the reasons for this is the government of Kuwait is extremely generous to their people. According to a Reuters article from 2013 ('Kuwait's parliament approves personal debt relief law'), in 1991, following the Gulf War, the government wrote off the majority of consumer debt and instigated a series of handouts to help restart life in the country. It then forgave $20 billion in bad loans still hanging around from the 1982 stock market crash where investors had borrowed large sums of money to invest in stocks. In 2011, to celebrate significant anniversaries, each Kuwaiti was given 1000 dinars and free food rations for 13 months. Even as recently as 2013, the parliament decided that the banks were accumulating their interest in an unfair way so approved a law to buy some citizens' personal loans and write off the interest. Add to all this the regular handouts of cash and benefits Kuwaitis get for significant events like having a child, getting married or finding yourself without a job, and you can start to see struggle and challenge is a distant memory for most Kuwaitis. The concept of competition has also been removed, through a government mandate to hire everyone. Everyone gets a job—if you graduate at 21, you have a job by 21 and 2 days. As a result of these measures, the majority of Kuwaitis are not striving. They are well looked after.

While I was there I spent a lot of time talking to expats about this issue. A number of them told me that Kuwaiti nationals who are employed by the government physically work on average between one and five hours per week. That is if they show up at all! Many of them mentioned people who are employed but didn't actually come to work—Kuwaiti nationals are often employed because they know someone of significance, but they are not required to come in at all. In fact, one manager told me that he had a woman in his team, on full pay and benefits, who had never even been to Kuwait and lived in Zürich.

Now, you might be reading this and thinking, *Regular handouts, no stress, don't have to go to work; bring that on!* However, this lack of challenge and struggle has robbed many of the beautiful people of Kuwait from living a fulfilled and purposeful life. Even the 18-year-old with the enviable car collection (who was a lovely guy, very kind and generous and not pretentious). When I spoke to him about his passions, his plans for the future and what made him feel alive, he simply talked about possessions and things that he had or wanted to buy.

The other thing I discovered is that the generosity and low challenge environment of Kuwait reduced peoples' autonomy and control over their own life. Many people I spoke to talked about simply following this path of generosity rather than choosing their own path in life because they would have to be foolish to say no to all this great stuff. One young woman I spoke to talked about how she was not living the life that she wanted to live because these amazing opportunities kept falling into her lap and she would feel silly and ungrateful to not accept them. The cost to her was that her dreams and passions got pushed to the side because the easy path simply made more sense. Just to clarify, this was not about suppression of a gender; I never found Kuwait to be oppressive of women. On the University campuses I saw more women than I did men, and some of the most intelligent and insightful questions I have ever got as a presenter came from Kuwaiti women. Rather, the problem came from a society that looked after her so well, it simply didn't seem to make sense to give up that easy path in search of a dream that would involve discomfort, uncertainty and struggle. All this generosity made many people more passive than active, removed their autonomy, and had them believing something else will take care of their lives and that they are not in control. When I said earlier that a certain percentage of the population lacked fire, this is the group I am referring to.

How does paradise sound now?

The good news is that my most recent research and interviews suggest that Kuwait is going through a transformation. More and more people are being proactive and taking action to improve their wellbeing, happiness and levels of positivity. Also, there is a new

Kuwait emerging, where people are striving, evolving and taking on challenge. In particular we have seen an explosion of young people focusing on entrepreneurial endeavours. They are helping Kuwait forge new paths in the areas of filmmaking, music, food, graphic design and technology. To do this these people are having to let go of the safety rope and forge their own path. This obviously brings uncertainty, challenge and struggle for them. Yet this group is displaying higher levels of fulfilment and zest for life. One young Kuwaiti was following a very successful career path and was on track for an executive role in a bank. He abandoned this safe and low risk plan and went off to become a chef. Whilst he admitted that this plan was risky and at many moments was extremely uncomfortable, he talked about how he had never felt so energised and awakened.

To summarise our findings, what this project taught us was that those who had what most people would consider the optimal life (low on challenge and struggle) lacked wellbeing, zest and passion. In contrast those who moved away from that seemingly low struggle environment into one that involved challenge, discomfort and uncertainty, became more alive and fulfilled.

What is good for us sounds counterintuitive

For more than a decade we have been obsessed with happiness. Thousands of books, presenters and courses are teaching us how to be happy. Are we more happy? No! We are the most depressed, anxious and medicated group of people in history. The happiness movement has failed us. It is detracting from our wellbeing, not adding to it. How has it done this? By demonising emotional states that do not align to happiness.

Struggle, challenge and discomfort are critical experiences human beings need so they can evolve and feel fulfilled.

Struggle, challenge and discomfort are critical experiences human beings need so they can evolve and feel fulfilled. As a society we have been approaching struggle, challenge and happiness all wrong. We can still have high levels of challenge and pressure and at the same time have excellent wellbeing and fulfilment. Our studies have shown that, just like the people of Kuwait, when we get everything we want, it's devastating for us.

Who were our guinea pigs?

As I've already mentioned, underpinning this book is ten years of research focusing on performance and wellbeing. The research did not focus on elite athletes or special forces soldiers. Why? Because they are freaks. They are not normal. They are so exceptional that many of the strategies they rely on do not relate to the average person. And our data set did not focus on CEOs of Fortune 500 companies, because they are freaks too. Many of them can sleep five hours a night and easily handle abnormal levels of stress and pressure. Plus, you don't want to emulate people who are elite. Why? In my experience, the majority of them are a disaster, often self-absorbed and unable to function in a constructive way.

Instead, this research focused on employees of varying levels of seniority. You could say we explored people at all levels of performance who had a 'normal' life. Although I also talk about Olympic athletes if their case study adds to the learning, they were not our focus and we did not build research around the 'find what the best of the best do and then teach everyone to do that, model.

The meaning of life (yeah, we aim that high)

The key finding we discovered over those ten years was that people are most fulfilled and feel best about themselves when they are in a state of striving. Just to remind you, I define striving as taking deliberate action towards a meaningful goal, aspiration or vision. However, it's not just any type of action. The action must require people to evolve and exhibit courage in the face of struggle.

Striving is made up of courage and evolution and it is the state you need to spend more time in if you want to live your best possible life.

So are you ready? On your marks, get set, go!

CHAPTER 1

Could everyone please shut up about happiness?

My aim is to help people become more fulfilled and evolved versions of themselves. While this might sound counterintuitive, one of the biggest blocks to people achieving this is their overwhelming and all-consuming desire to be happy. And I don't mean just experiencing the emotion of happiness. In society today we interpret happiness as no longer being an emotion but rather a perpetual state of comfort that avoids negative emotion. We want to evolve and grow and innovate—as long as it can be a comfortable process. I see this in organisations all the time. They want to take risks, just as long as they can control everything and ensure it will feel comfortable and avoid any chance of failure. I use the terms 'happiness', 'comfort' and 'feeling good' interchangeably in this book. When I do that, what I'm referring to is our desire to avoid struggle.

An important point to make is that I am not anti-joy or happiness. I think they're great. I am not the happiness Grinch. (I haven't even seen either of the movies.) Joy is one of my most favourite emotions and I believe cultivating positive emotion in our lives is important. By all means, seek out happiness and joy. Do things and surround yourself with people who bring you both. However, be mindful of when happiness is not serving you. In some contexts, we have gone too far with the desire to be happy all the time—and it's come back to bite us on the arse.

The happiness movement has become massively dysfunctional for three reasons: we now think we need to be constantly happy, we feel guilty about negative emotion, and we're not evolving. Let's look at each of these in turn.

We want happiness to be our constant state

People today expect to feel good all the time. When they don't, they think something is wrong with them or their life. The problem is happiness is an emotion, and emotions come and go. Sadness, rage, jealousy, embarrassment, enthusiasm and delight—they come in, do a job, which is to steer our behaviour in a certain direction, and then they leave. This is how we were designed and it's a great system. But we have messed with the system. We picked one emotion (happiness) and said this should be our constant state. Happiness in itself has become the goal. Feeling a constant state of happiness, however, is physiologically and psychologically impossible. It just can't happen. This expectation of perpetual happiness is not only delusional, it is also fraught with disaster. All too often we freak out and beat ourselves up about the fact that we are not experiencing enough happiness. Comparing ourselves to others does not help here and nor does social media bombarding us with images of all our friends being delighted, often leading us to feel inadequate.

> **Feeling a constant state of happiness is physiologically and psychologically impossible.**

Instead, a far healthier frame is to think of emotions as swings of a golf club. (Stay with me here and let me explain.) I am a terrible golfer but when I play golf I don't beat myself up about how many swings I take because my view is that the more swings I take at the ball, the more value for money I have gotten. The purpose I see for golf is to hit the ball. If I hit the ball twice as many times as a friend of mine, I have received twice the return on my investment. Look at emotions the same way. To get the most out of life you want to feel a whole range of different emotions, both positive and negative. The meaning of life is to experience as many things as possible and we should put emotions in that category as well.

A mate of mine, Todd Kashdan, co-authored a book with Robert Biswas-Diener called *The Upside of Your Dark Side*, where they very elegantly point out the importance of experiencing a range of emotions, including negative emotion (such as fear, jealously, anger, disappointment). They argue that negative emotion is often a signal you have made a mistake and a correction is needed. They also demonstrate in many cases positive emotion like happiness can be incredibly dysfunctional in the wrong context. For example, if you have to do a very important task, the fear and anxiety you naturally feel will help you to focus and put in your best effort. In contrast, if you repress that anxiety and are overly optimistic about your chances of completing it you may bring more of a blasé and careless approach.

Key message people: stop thinking you have to feel happy all the time.

JOY, SADNESS AND DYSFUNCTION

If you'd like some popular culture to back up my point about seeking a constant state of happiness, check out the children's movie *Inside Out*. It is a brilliant example of what can happen when we prioritise one emotion to the point of suppressing others. The story is set inside the brain of a young girl (Riley) when she goes through a difficult stage in her life. The main characters are five different emotions, Joy, Fear, Anger, Disgust and Sadness. Joy is a control freak and tries to run the show and dominate. In particular, Joy won't let Riley feel sadness. As the movie unfolds, Joy's actions lead to huge dysfunction and Riley's life falls apart. By the end of the movie, Joy learns that for Riley to have a full life, she needs to feel a whole range of emotions, not just the ones that feel good.

Even negative emotions have benefits

I use negative thinking and emotion to be a better dad. As I get home at the end of the day, I take a moment to think, *What if this was the last time I ever saw my family? What if they had a terrible accident tomorrow and they were wiped off the earth?* Now that might seem like some weird, morbid shit, and it probably is. However, those negative thoughts and emotions put me in a headspace of gratitude and engagement, which improves my behaviour. Being a good dad is about displaying better behaviours so, regardless of how I got there, I got there.

I use this strategy in many situations at home, such as after reading my daughters stories and they ask me to climb up into their bunk beds and give them a cuddle, for the third time that night. Rather than thinking I've had a long day and I just want to go zone out, I think how many years I have left where my daughters ask me to climb into bed and give them a cuddle. These negative thoughts and emotions help me enjoy the moment and display better behaviours. Negative emotions and thoughts can be incredibly helpful and constructive, so don't feel bad for experiencing them.

Don't panic when sadness comes knocking

In January 2019, I was preparing to go back to work after my regular summer break from work. Over the Christmas period I tend to take three to four weeks off to totally switch off from work and immerse myself in my family and friends. I love this time off so much and it sets me up for the upcoming year. Joy, fun and relaxation are the words I would use to describe it. The last week of the holiday is always a little stressful as I think about going back to work, but this year my mood and mindset crashed to a new low.

I don't know what happened but I was engulfed in an incredible amount of sadness and dread, which I had never experienced before. I felt like a dark cloud was strangling the life out of me. My mood fluctuated between rage, frustration, sadness and despair. I had never felt so terrible. I found it hard to interact with people, especially my family. I just wanted to curl up in bed and remove myself from the world. I even had suicidal thoughts on occasion and thought, *What is the point of going on if this is what life is going to be like?*

To deal with it all, I sat down and started to write out all the thoughts and emotions that were going through my head. To say the least, my notes were pretty dark and concerning. But after getting it all out on paper, I came up with four focuses:

1. *Don't freak out.* This didn't mean my life was over and I had some sort of big problem. It could simply be a transient low mood. Rather than panic and catastrophise, I sat with the discomfort and focused on what better behaviours I could do to reduce the impact of this situation on my life. (Obviously if this mood had continued for an extended period of time, I would have sought professional help.)

2. *Don't act on the impulses I felt.* I wanted to take my mood out on other people, blame them, yell and scream, and be petty. I was channelling a three year old, mid-tantrum. I was aware of these impulses and how dysfunctional they were. When they came up in the moment, I focused on just shutting my mouth and not reacting.

3. *Do behaviours that helped me feel better.* Even though I didn't feel like it, I dialled up how much exercise I was doing, spent more time in nature, increased how much meditation I was doing, and swam in the ocean. At one point, my wife sent me on a very long drive—probably more for her benefit than mine.

4. *Do turn to a couple of good mates.* I chatted to them about what I was going through, and talking about it really reduced the shame and fear that I felt. Without fail, each of them said, 'I hear you. I have been there'. That was amazingly powerful.

With these habits in place I sat in the discomfort and almost brought a level of curiosity to my terrible state, rather than slipping into panic. I became more like, *Wow I am feeling really bad. I have never felt like this before. What is causing it? What things are making me feel better?*

About a week after the dark cloud of sadness appeared, it suddenly left and I felt instantly better—and I have not retreated back there since. If I analyse this whole situation, the most helpful thing I did was not panic about my sadness. Rather, I accepted my mood and focused on constructive behaviours that would improve the impact I had on myself and others.

We feel guilty for experiencing and expressing negative emotion

The desire to feel happy all the time has resulted in social pressure to deny our negative emotional state. We are expected to express positive emotion constantly and, if we don't, we are somehow being ungrateful for all the great things we have. While you don't want to be an annoying douche bag that complains about trivial things, it seems no longer acceptable to be annoyed and frustrated anymore. Experiencing negative emotion has become socially unacceptable.

#firstworldproblems

I had been on the road for a couple of days and was looking forward to making it home so I could have dinner with my family. My flight had already been delayed by two hours and when we finally boarded we sat on the tarmac for another 90 minutes. I was no longer going to make dinner but I could make it in time to read my girls a story before they fell asleep—that was until it took 45 minutes for my bag to come out after we landed. I was tired and frustrated and, most importantly, I was going to miss seeing my daughters before they fell asleep. Feeling alone and sad I vented my frustration on Facebook. (You know how bad things have become when you turn to Facebook for comfort and validation.)

In response to my post one of my Facebook 'friends' commented, 'I'm sure there's far worse things that could happen to you mate #firstworldproblems'.

My reply was (after deleting my first reply, which would have made Gordon Ramsay blush),

Hate it when people say first world problems. Arriving 4 hours later than I am supposed to sucks and has really pissed me off. Why do we have to be positive about everything?

To which they replied,

A friend of mine and her 2 kids said goodbye to her husband and their dad as he went to WA on a business trip. He died in the hotel the next morning. Perhaps I should have said #perspective.

Now I was really pissed off, I hate that guilt bullshit. So I replied,

Why can't you just say 'that sucks you don't get to have dinner with your wife and kids after a long week away'? Why do we feel the need to tell people that they can't feel an emotion because someone has it worse off? Is it really that damaging to be annoyed? I think this illustrates why the self-help, be always positive world is so messed up. My perspective is fine. I am just experiencing the emotion of frustration and sadness!

What this illustrates (apart from the fact that I should stay off Facebook), is that all too often we shame people for feeling negative emotion.

This type of response increases our guilt around feeling negative emotions and leads us to seeing them as bad and something we need to repress or replace with more positive emotions. It also stops people expressing how they truly feel. Rather than judgement and the, 'You think that's bad ...' response when they express discomfort, a far more healthy and helpful response is to display empathy.

In support of this, in their article 'The poverty of privilege', therapists JL Wolfe and IG Fodor report that people from affluent backgrounds—whose lives seem perfect on paper—experience a huge feeling of shame in expressing any level of unhappiness or negative emotion. They fear being judged as ungrateful and self-indulgent if they complain about their privileged lives.

And in 'The culture of affluence' Suniya Luthar reports that teens from privileged families feel judgement rather than support if they disclose a feeling of being unhappy. When they shared with others that they felt depressed, many teens said those people dismissed their feelings with a reaction of 'what could you possibly have to complain about? Don't you know there are starving children in Africa?' (My grandmother loved to roll that one out.) Some even reacted with anger and saw the unhappy privileged child as self-centred and ungrateful. When people share their feelings with others and receive this reaction, their level of negative emotion is only exacerbated. Soon they stop expressing what is going on for them and instead push those feelings deep down inside, which leads to all sorts of terrible dysfunction.

Seeking happiness stops us from evolving

Finally, the desire to feel good holds us back from doing the things that challenge us to evolve and grow. This links in with my main message (that self-esteem and fulfilment comes from courageously striving through struggle and challenge) and is the biggest dysfunction that results from the happiness movement.

What we know about evolution and change is that it feels bad. It feels scary, unsettling and uncertain. In business today, people talk about innovation like it's some sort of fun process. Innovation is not fun! Innovation is a process rich in vulnerability and it is inherently uncomfortable. If it feels good, it's not innovation. However, if we have happiness as our objective and greatest desire, when we go through change and we experience uncomfortable emotions, our natural reaction is to retreat from that change. As a result, we retreat back to old safe behaviours that bring back the happiness but do not result in us evolving and growing.

> **Innovation is not fun! Innovation is a process rich in vulnerability and it is inherently uncomfortable. If it feels good, it's not innovation.**

The constant desire to experience happiness is one of the biggest blocks to progress, and we saw this on a daily basis in our research. Leaders would attempt to exhibit new and challenging behaviours (that would help evolve their leadership and transform the company), but these actions would bring up uncomfortable thoughts and emotions and, in an attempt to make them go away, the leaders would abandon their change efforts. We also witnessed this in team members wanting to try new and different behaviours.

The continual search for happiness has perverted our relationship with discomfort, challenge and struggle. The fallout of this is that we avoid these uncomfortable states and move towards comfort and pleasure. This mindset greatly limits our evolution and development. A full and meaningful life will be fraught with uncomfortable emotions. If you are truly doing the clichéd thing of 'sucking the marrow out of life', schedule in dealing with a boatload of uncomfortable emotions. The key here is to develop the self-awareness to understand when the desire for happiness is hooking you into behaviours that lead you away from evolution and growth. From our interviews, one of people's greatest frustrations and disappointments was that when negative emotion showed up they did not meet it with courage but rather let the desire to feel good drive them into avoidance.

A new lens to look at happiness through

Instead of being the sole objective, happiness should be the by-product of a life spent striving to grow and evolve. Rather than focusing on happiness, focusing on fulfilment is more advantageous.

> **Rather than focusing on happiness, focusing on fulfilment is more advantageous.**

Are you fulfilled in life? Are you evolving as a person? Are you living aligned to your values? Are you contributing to something bigger than yourself? Are you being courageous? Do you stand for something? What are your relationships like? How do you express love and care for the people and world around you?

Our obsession with experiencing happiness has brainwashed us with the view that we must think positive thoughts, and we must be flooded with positive emotions and attitudes. And so we focus on doing tasks that leverage our strengths to be in a state of contentment. This mindset stops us from getting in the trenches with struggle and challenge.

In her 2004 paper 'The negative side of positive psychology', Barbara Held argues, people often have to face hardships and difficulties that they cannot transcend and get over, or look at in a positive way no matter what they do. As Held highlights,

> **If they buy into the happiness myth they will end up feeling even worse; they could feel guilty or defective for not having the right (positive) attitude, in addition to whatever was ailing them in the first place.**

Moreover, she also argues that emotions, and whether they are good or bad, have become polarising. We have been force-fed the incorrect message of, 'Positivity is good and good for you; negativity is bad and bad for you'.

I am not saying happiness is not worth pursuing; however, we have applied it to our lives with a far too wide brush. For too many years, psychology only focused on pathology and dysfunction but now the pendulum has swung back excessively. We have to have a more measured approach to happiness and positive emotion. Humans are complex creatures and, as a result, need a more complex approach to their psychological and emotional states, one that takes in the importance of fulfilment.

SUMMARY

- Our obsession with happiness has become too extreme and is now having a negative impact on our lives in the following ways:

  - We expect happiness to be a constant state. This is unobtainable and causes us to miss out on the benefits of negative emotion.

  - We feel guilty for experiencing negative emotion. We feel pressure to consistently experience and exhibit positive emotion.

  - An overemphasis on seeking happiness encourages us to retreat from struggle, discomfort and challenge. This limits our ability to evolve and grow.

- Rather than focusing on happiness, focusing on fulfilment is more advantageous. Are you fulfilled in life? Are you evolving as a person? Are you living aligned to your values? Are you contributing to something bigger than yourself? Are you being courageous? Do you stand for something? Happiness is a by-product of living a fulfilled life.

CHAPTER 2

The completion myth

Before I get into the nuts and bolts of how you can effectively strive, I need to clear up a misconception about goals and achievement and the completion myth. What I mean by that is the misconception that in the process of working towards a goal, aspiration or vision, you experience the most amount of satisfaction when you finally achieve the end result.

Let me explain. Typically, we set a goal (complete a marathon), aspiration (be a compassionate and calm parent) or vision for our life (I want to run my own successful small business), and from there our focus becomes arriving at the goal, aspiration or vision, seeing the striving part as the section we have to tolerate and suffer through. As summed up in the following figure, we are conditioned to think we will love the achieving part and at best endure the striving section.

In contrast to this strongly held view, my team's research showed that people felt most alive and stimulated in the striving period leading up to the goal. Completing the goal did produce a period of elation, but this was followed by a flat spot of indifference, disappointment and often sadness, during which people are grieving that they are no longer in the striving phase. The completion of the goal has taken the striving away and an emptiness ensues.

If I had a dollar for every person I have worked with who said 'Wow I achieved that goal and now I feel so flat. I thought I'd feel elated but I just feel...flat', I would have at least \$67. Probably more. It's not the achievement that makes us feel alive but the striving and seeking. While this sounds counterintuitive, we are most alive when we are in the trenches overcoming difficult obstacles. We feel best about ourselves when we are being courageous and evolving while progressing towards a goal, not when we arrive at the goal, as shown in the next figure.

We feel best about ourselves when we are being courageous and evolving while progressing towards a goal, not when we arrive at the goal.

Seeking versus finding

In 2016, Olivia Goldhill wrote a brilliant article featured on one of my favourite websites Quartz (www.qz.com), titled 'Neuroscience confirms that to be truly happy, you will always need something more'.

Goldhill writes about the neuroscientist Jaak Panksepp who suggests that of the seven core instincts in the human brain (anger, fear, panic-grief, maternal care, pleasure/lust, play, and seeking), seeking (or what I call striving) is the most vital. All of us have this desire to seek, fed by the neurotransmitter dopamine. When we seek, we are rewarded by our brain being flooded with dopamine which, in turn, makes us feel pleasure. As Goldhill notes,

> The human desire to seek explains why achieving major goals, or even winning the lottery, doesn't cause long-term changes in happiness. But our drive to look ahead needn't cause a permanent state of dissatisfaction, as seeking is itself a fulfilling activity.

In other words, the goal is not the goal. The striving towards the goal is the goal. The moment we achieve a milestone, our seeking drive kicks back in to keep us moving on to the next milestone.

Jaak Panskepp is also quoted in the HuffPost article 'Depressed? Your "SEEKING" system might not be working', where he states, 'typically it's not the reward that makes us feel euphoric, but the search itself'. Panksepp argues that when we are no longer striving, our life falls into a downward spiral and that the opposite of striving is depression.

His research reinforces the importance of striving. Unfortunately, however, society has conditioned us to totally buy into the completion myth. We see success as a binary process. We either hit the goal or we didn't. But working towards achieving a goal is multi-dimensional, and goals are more sophisticated and nuanced than the black and white view we have. We must factor in the striving part of goal acquisition because in this phase comes tremendous growth, even if we don't achieve the goal.

> The goal is not the goal. The striving towards the goal is the goal.

When we asked our research participants what the most desirable and satisfying part of a goal was, they almost universally said its achievement. However, their diary entries, where they reflected in the moment and where we asked them to reflect on the different stages of a goal, told a very different story. The data here showed that the striving section was where the good stuff lived. People talked about having to draw on their internal resources to overcome unsuspected challenges, or seeing their team come together in a cohesive fashion to solve a problem that everyone thought was impossible. They talked about having to dig in and not give up, even when they doubted their ability.

I also see this in my own life. I was running the concept of this book by a friend of mine, Nicole, when she said, 'I have been living this'. She had just completed a half-marathon a couple of weeks before and said, 'When I finished the race, I was thrilled and felt on top of the world for a couple of days. But very quickly I started to miss having that goal to work towards and I had this sense of emptiness. Two days ago I signed up for the New York marathon and the moment I did I started to feel alive again. Also, after reflecting on the whole experience, I realised that I was most proud of the training I put in, how consistent I was, how I overcame the injuries I got, how hard I worked at my rehab. I was proud of how tough and consistent I was in my training more than the fact that I finished the race.'

I started to see the relationship between challenge and feeling alive everywhere. I caught up with Tony, a friend of mine who runs a very successful property company. He had recently achieved a huge business milestone he had been working towards for years. In addition, he had just bought his dream car and built his dream house. Rather than skipping through the door, however, he dragged his feet. He said, 'I really expected to be elated when we hit that target. But I just feel flat and lost. I am kind of looking around thinking, what's next?'

And this applies to all levels of success. I was honoured to speak at a conference with Tony Hsieh, founder of online shoe store Zappos, which was sold to Amazon for a cool one billion dollars. Just take a moment for that to sink in: one BBBBBBBillion dollars. Chatting to Tony, he told me the story of when Microsoft bought his first company for $265 million. He said, 'We were having coffee when we got the message that the deal was done and the money had been transferred into our account. I thought I would have been ecstatic, but I felt grief and loss. I realised what I loved was building the company, building a team and solving the problems. Rather than looking at my bank balance and thinking, *This will bring me so much happiness!*, I saw it as taking me away from the things that lit me up inside'.

The hedonic treadmill is not found at the gym

Additional research that backs up the idea of the completion myth looks at what's been termed the 'hedonic treadmill'. While at first impression this may sound like Kim Kardashian using exercise equipment, it is a genuine psychological concept sometimes also referred to as 'hedonic adaptation'. Basically, the idea argues that humans return back to a relatively stable level of happiness, despite the experience of significant positive or negative events or changes in life. In other words, good and bad events temporarily affect happiness, but people quickly adapt back to their stable set point of happiness. This theory shows us that individual and societal efforts to increase happiness are futile. (Yeah, this is the motivational feel good part of the book.)

Despite this finding, people continue to pursue happiness because they incorrectly believe that greater happiness lies just around the corner—in the next goal accomplished, the next social relationship obtained, or the next problem solved. They get stuck on this treadmill of constantly thinking that the next milestone will grant them the gift of happiness, without realising that in the long run such activity will never deliver on its promise.

As David Myers stated in his 1992 book *The Pursuit of Happyness*,

> The point cannot be overstated: Every desirable experience — passionate love, a spiritual high, the pleasure of a new possession, the exhilaration of success — is transitory.

Psychologists have supported these arguments, showing that after people achieve a certain level of affluence, they very rapidly become habituated to this and then place their gaze on achieving a new and higher level of affluence. A huge amount of data shows that people with enormous amounts of money are actually no happier than their less wealthy counterparts, and they are statistically more prone to depression and other forms of mental health.

And in their paper 'Beyond money: Toward an economy of well-being', Ed Diener and Martin Seligman report that,

> Over the past 50 years, income has climbed steadily in the United States, with the gross domestic product (GDP) per capita tripling, and yet life satisfaction has been virtually flat.

Despite this rise in income, measures of ill-being are increasing. As shown by Jean Twenge in 'The age of anxiety', depression rates have increased ten-fold over the same 50-year period, and rates of anxiety are also rising. Twenge highlights the average American child in the 1980s reported greater anxiety than the average child receiving psychiatric treatment in the 1950s. Holy shit, what have we done to our kids?

When it comes to cars, I am the walking embodiment of the hedonic treadmill. About five years ago I achieved a significant business milestone and my wife suggested I reward myself. Not needing to be told twice, I went out and I bought my dream car, a Mercedes

AMG. (I told you I am a tragic car guy.) However, three months later I was searching YouTube for the car I would buy next. I know what you're thinking and the answer is yes. I am a wanker. But I blame the hedonic treadmill. Once I had the thing I had been wanting for years, my thoughts turned to, *What's next?*

In my defence, evidence shows that spending money on an experience in comparison to a possession leads to more sustained levels of happiness. Dr Tom Gilovich, a researcher from Cornell University points out that an experience has multiple facets. A holiday, for example, involves the planning of the trip, the anticipation of the experience, the actual experience, the reliving and sharing with others of it afterwards and the memories that pop up for you for years to come. In contrast, a possession doesn't have those sustainable layers and is far more transactional and so does not live on. In addition, Dr Gilovich showed that leading up to an experience people felt excitement and anticipation, while people waiting for something they ordered primarily felt impatience.

The dangers of the completion myth

Buying into the completion myth is dangerous for two reasons. Firstly, because obsessing about the outcome means we miss out on the enjoyment, development and lessons learned in the strive. We are blind to the gifts that exist in the trenches. Secondly, when we fully buy into the completion myth, the crash on the other side of achievement becomes even deeper. If you believe achieving the goal means your life will be amazing and perfect and easy from then on in, the impact on your mental health can be devastating.

I saw this a lot in athletes, and in particular following an Olympics where they won a medal. They had spent years training with a single focus and, when it was achieved, the feeling on the other side was nothing like they expected. They came home with a gold medal believing that the world would fall at their feet. But after a couple of weeks, the interviews finish, the parties are over and they are left without the strive and a painfully empty feeling. If they are not careful, it can eat them up inside. In the research for the book, I interviewed two gold medallists (they asked not to be mentioned by name because the pain is still very real and raw for them). They both said the period of two to six months after coming home was very dark for them. One said they got heavily into drinking and recreational drugs to numb the discomfort. He actually went as far as losing his gold medal while on a drunken night out. Their families talked about how hard that period was and how genuinely worried they were for them.

In addition, I've spoken to a number of elite athletes about what it's like to retire. Very similar themes come up, and they talk about how devastatingly difficult it is to move on from that part of their life. What is interesting is that one of the things they miss the most is the training, the structure, the comradery with their teammates and the dedication they have to exhibit.

MIKE PAGAN ON RETIREMENT

Mike Pagan is a performance coach and speaker specialising in the support of elite sportspeople and business professionals in transition, in particular retirement. Mike told me that when an athlete retires, three big things can happen:

1. *Their support network disappears.* If you are a high-level athlete, you have a cast of thousands looking after you, including coach, manager, sports psychologist, nutritionist, and finance and PR managers. When you retire, they all move on to other athletes.

2. *Their identity shifts.* Retired athletes suddenly become someone who used to be an athlete, someone who used to be famous. No-one screams their name from the crowd anymore. They don't know who they are and how they fit into the world.

> 3. *They miss the strive.* This relates most strongly to the theme
> of the book. Mike said,
>
> What devastates the athletes so much is that they miss the striving for
> that extra millisecond, that extra millimetre. They miss the obsession
> with achieving mastery and evolving. The discipline and focus required to
> show up at each training session and continually progress makes them a
> better version of themselves. This is one of the reasons many athletes have
> relationship and behavioural issues after they retire.
>
> **Finally, Mike told me,**
>
> The athletes who do really well in retirement have great support networks
> and find that new thing they are working towards. They have clarity around
> the next challenging thing they are striving towards that has meaning and
> purpose attached to it.

A couple of years ago I had the pleasure of doing a speaking road
show with Shane Webcke. Shane was a professional rugby league
footballer who played prop forward for the Brisbane Broncos. He is
considered to be one of the greatest forwards to ever play the game.
The guy's achievements could fill a book on their own, including
playing for Australia 26 times and for Queensland 21 times in the
State of Origin series.

What struck me about Shane, apart from the fact that he is a
cracking human being and was very generous with his time, is that
he's incredibly articulate, very bright and a deep thinker. One of
the many conversations we had on the road show was around how
difficult he'd found retirement from football. He told me, 'It was ten
times harder than I thought it would be and no-one prepared me for
it. After I retired, I caught up with a few other blokes who retired at
the same time as me and they were really struggling. Retirement was
like falling off a cliff.' While writing the book I called him to get some
deeper insights on how he coped with it.

SHANE WEBCKE ON RETIREMENT

Here's what Shane told me:

I never for one minute missed the adulation or people cheering my name or the applause; that never held a lot of appeal for me. What I missed was the order and regime and purpose that being a professional athlete brought. The routine of having to go to training or to play and the discipline of expecting more from yourself every day, pushing yourself to be the best you can be was what I found so fulfilling. Straight after I retired, people kept telling me to rest and take it easy. But that only made it worse. I didn't need rest; I needed to find the next thing I would throw myself into.

That's what I did. I picked two things, public speaking and presenting on TV. Both of those things I found super challenging but I thought, *Stuff it. I really want to get good at them.* They weren't things that I was super passionate about. In fact, I didn't enjoy them at the start, and many times I hated it and thought about quitting. But I just focused on the challenge and I thought this is not going to beat me, I will master them.

Taking action was the key; I took action even when I felt like crap. My greatest passion in life is the farm I own and within that I took risks, I tried new things and I really stretched myself. It was the challenge involved in those three activities that made me feel alive again. For about two years after I retired I just didn't feel good, I felt lost. I only started to feel better when I had this full, demanding and challenging life. That's when I got my mojo back. Today I am as busy as when I was a full-time athlete. The way I view it is I haven't retired, I have just changed jobs.

My advice to anyone who is struggling is get into something; throw yourself into some sort of challenging activity. The biggest mistake people make is to wait for the thing that they think they will have a passion for for the rest of their life. It doesn't have to be perfect. Find yourself a new routine, find yourself some pressure, find yourself obligation. When you don't have those three things, you feel messed up.

Shane is also a true champion of people in the bush, and does a tremendous amount of work to help the rural community. In our

> discussion, he talked about the many challenges and hardships he has seen people go through. He said,
>
> The people who get through these hard times, what they have in common is they keep moving, whether they feel good, bad or indifferent. On any given day, you get up and you do what you have to do. But in this happiness obsessed world apparently it's a bad thing if you have a bad day or you feel poorly, or you have pressure or you have dramas or you don't feel quite yourself. Too many people today think that feeling that way is terrible. Life will never be even or kind. It is our ability to keep moving forward, good, bad or indifferent, that is the thing that allows us to have a fulfilling life.
>
> **Rock on, Shane — brilliant advice!**

My conversations with Shane cemented what our research had found. Too often we see the uncomfortable feelings as a reason to not take action, and are instead waiting to feel good before we can change. Shane highlighting the importance of routine and obligation was also backed up by the interviews I did with retired people, the long-term unemployed and welfare workers. One welfare worker told me, 'With the people I work with, I simply focus on having them get up at a reasonable time, get showered, get dressed and leave the house to go do something by 9 am. This simple routine can be transformative for people who are dependent on welfare; it starts to shift their mentality and wellbeing'.

Again, the strive can be transformative regardless of the outcome. One of my closest friends was a successful bodybuilder who suffered from severe obsessive compulsive disorder. How his OCD manifested itself was not in that he had to turn the light on and off 50 times before he could leave the house, or wash his hands compulsively. His OCD was around obsessive thoughts, which could scream inside his head. This obviously had a debilitating impact on his quality of life and relationships. Interestingly the happiest and most functional I ever saw him was when he was preparing for a bodybuilding competition, which would begin 12 to 16 weeks out from the competition. For that period of time, the preparation basically consumes a bodybuilder's life. It is a combination of training with weights, often twice a day, doing cardio and being insanely meticulous with your diet.

My friend confirmed what I had observed, saying to me, 'I'm always happiest in comp prep. I have such clear purpose and I have to be focused on every aspect of the preparation. It is like those voices inside my head quiet down for that period of time. The worst part is when the comp's over. I fall into post-comp blues and the voices return'.

Avoiding the completion myth trap

So how do you not fall into the completion myth trap? In two (not so easy) steps.

Step 1: Be aware

The first step is a simple one to understand but a difficult one to carry out. It is to be aware of when you're falling into the completion myth trap. Realise that the achievement of the goal does not hold all the fulfilment. Rather, the striving in the lead-up to the goal really makes you feel alive. By all means celebrate the victory, savour the moment and soak it up but don't resent, skip over or miss the learnings that sit within the strive. Also, and most importantly, don't believe the bullshit that we have been fed around thinking that at the point of achievement the clouds will part, the angels will sing and you will be delivered into a place of transcendence where you have 'arrived'—and life will be beer and skittles afterwards. Slap yourself if you ever hear anything like the following come out of your mouth:

- When I have a relationship, I will...
- When I get the promotion...
- When the kids leave home...
- When I retire...
- When I start loving myself...

> **The achievement of the goal does not hold all the fulfilment. Rather, the striving in the lead-up to the goal really makes you feel alive.**

The statement 'When I' followed by some sort of achievement, followed then by a future state that is most commonly seen at the end of romantic movies is a fast track to disappointment.

Instead, happiness and fulfilment live in the strive.

Step 2: Fall in love with the work

One of my favourite shows is Jerry Seinfeld's *Comedians in cars getting coffee*. Each episode, Jerry meets up with a comedian and they go for coffee in an exotic car (probably didn't have to spell that out for you because the title kind of gives it away). In one episode, Jerry meets with Barack Obama. I know you are thinking, he's the president not a comedian. But as Jerry points out at the start of the show, Obama has pulled off enough gags in his time to qualify as a comedian. They are having coffee when Jerry asks Obama what percentage of world leaders are completely out of their mind—to which Obama responds, 'a pretty sizeable percentage'.

The conversation then turns to how to keep perspective and stay grounded. At this point, Obama turns to Jerry and asks, 'How have you done it? You have one of the most successful TV shows in history, you have fame and ridiculous amounts of money, yet you seem relatively normal. How have you kept perspective?' Jerry's response is one of the most beautiful lines I have ever heard: he says, 'Because I fell in love with the work.

> **You gotta fall in love with the work.**

The work was joyful and difficult and interesting and that was my focus'. There you go people, striving in action. You gotta fall in love with the work.

THE STRIVE

GOAL
VISION
ASPIRATION

FALL in LOVE with the WORK
THIS is WHERE the GOLD SITS

GETTING EVERYTHING
YOU WANT IS
HARMFUL
TO YOU!

Don't learn from
negative emotion

Guilty for
feeling unhappy

We run from
discomfort

OUR OBSESSION with HAPPINESS has
LED to THESE DYSFUNCTIONS

SUMMARY

- After we achieve something, a period of flatness and disappointment always follows. Rarely does the achievement of a goal fulfil us in a way we expected.

- We feel most alive in the striving towards a goal rather than the achievement of the goal.

- Humans are hardwired to seek out the next challenge; it is in our DNA.

- We get used to what we have really, really fast and immediately start to look at what is next.

- Shane Webcke is a legend.

- Achieving a goal will not deliver eternal happiness, and we never really arrive.

- Don't ignore the strive. We often see this as the part we have to tolerate or put up with, but that is where the gold is.

- A key part to living a fulfilled life is to fall in love with the work.

CHAPTER 3

Easy sucks

From a marketing perspective the thing that striving has against it is that it involves struggle. The problem with struggle is that it brings along its friend discomfort. A far more appealing message to send out to people is that they will get a life that is pleasurable, full of positive emotion and free of discomfort. We are obsessed with comfort and it has made us allergic to discomfort. However, what my and my team's research shows is that things being too easy is devastating for human beings. We need life to be challenging. Put bluntly, 'Easy sucks'.

We won't sit with discomfort

The main reason we want our life to be easy is that not everyone has drunk the 'discomfort is good for me' Kool-Aid. In fact, it seems that we are no longer able to sit with discomfort in any form. Because we see discomfort as a bad thing, as soon as we feel it, we seem to have a knee-jerk reaction that propels us to try to get away from it. Unfortunately, our attempts to make the discomfort go away result in us often falling into dysfunctional behaviours. To find evidence of this, you just have to look at any political (or other) debate on social media and see how quickly it descends into name-calling and threatening language. Rather than following the impulse to make discomfort go away we need to have a more functional relationship with struggle. This is vitally important for business as our research is showing that the competitive advantage in business today is the ability to sit with discomfort, accept that it is a normal part of the change process and focus on the growth and development that comes from the struggle.

> The competitive advantage in business today is the ability to sit with discomfort ... and focus on the growth and development that comes from the struggle.

My first exposure to people's inability to sit with discomfort was when I was volunteering as a companion to the cancer charity Camp Quality. The role of a companion is to support and help families and children who are affected by cancer. In that time, some of the children I looked after and developed strong bonds with died. The death of a child can only be described in one way. It's totally fucked. It's not beautiful and it's not enlightening. Maybe someone more evolved than me can view it through a different lens but for me it just felt unfair and wrong. I still feel a mixture of rage and anguish whenever I think about it.

Because grief was something we encountered regularly in this role, Camp Quality was really great at giving us training around dealing with grief. One particular day, they brought in grief counsellor Mal McKissick, who is one of Australia's leading experts in this area. He won us over right from the start. Okay, he was actually 20 minutes late, which was not a great first impression, but when he arrived, he explained that he now specialised in counselling children who were going through grief. That day happened to be Father's Day and, while he apologised for being late, he also said, 'Some of the children I'm working with have lost their fathers and wanted to ring me to wish me a happy Father's Day, and that's not a call I'm gonna reject'. Apology accepted, Mal, say no more! We genuflect at your greatness.

Mal was masterful, engaging and so real. The biggest lesson he taught us that day was that when you are supporting someone in grief, you have to sit in the silence. You have to sit in the discomfort and shouldn't ever dare try to make your own discomfort go away. He talked about how incredibly hard this is to do. When most people are supporting someone in grief, they do and say things to try to make their own discomfort go away. But the result is they trivialise the other person's grief—and the grieving person can end up supporting them.

For example, say you go and see a friend who has lost someone they are close to and they are distraught. If you cannot sit with that discomfort, you end up saying things like, 'I don't know what to say, I feel so useless. I wish there was more I could do for you. I was worried about saying something stupid'. Because they don't want you to feel bad, they then start to say things like, 'I know, it's so hard. It's okay, I'll get through this' and they start to downplay their own grief and change their behaviour to make you feel better. The grieving person becomes the one who is doing the counselling. This dynamic leads to the person who needs support not getting their needs met—and all because you couldn't sit with the discomfort.

I saw this firsthand. At the funeral of a boy I had been a companion for, I witnessed countless people (who were as equally confronted as I was at the pain of losing a child and deeply uncomfortable with the strong feelings they were experiencing) tell the grieving parents to 'move on, be strong for their family; you have to think about your surviving children, they wouldn't want you to wallow and be miserable; keep living your life'. What drives this response from people is they don't want to be around negative emotion. Imagine if instead we could care for these parents by actually being there for them; if we could sit with our own uncomfortable feelings in a way that allows us to support them to express their grief in any way they deem appropriate, rather than encouraging and asking them to swallow and suppress their pain. Instead of judging people's reactions, we need to put our discomfort to the side and let them grieve in any way they deem appropriate.

This training has served me countless times throughout my life. I recently was at a funeral because one of my closest friends had lost her mother through suicide in a horrible set of circumstances. What made it even sadder, if that was humanly possible, was this woman was such a delight and such a gentle, kind soul. When I arrived, I saw my friend and walked up to her. There was a small line of people in front of me, all going up to her one by one and giving their condolences. As I was standing there, I could hear the things they were saying—things like, 'You have to be strong for your father', 'Your mother would want you to move on and not be so sad', 'You have a family now, don't let this distract you from them', 'Your mother is in heaven with the Lord. She is in a better place, so don't be angry that she is gone. This is part of God's plan'. While they were saying what they thought was the right thing to say and their intent was pure, they were not validating how she was feeling, and you could say they were using emotional blackmail to get her to calm down. People's desire for themselves to not witness or experience discomfort makes them interfere in and judge a person's very normal and healthy reaction to loss. Having said that, if I hadn't done the bereavement training with Mal, I would have said similar things.

Trying to avoid discomfort can lead us to doing very dysfunctional things that, while good intentioned, do not serve the situation. At the funeral, I just walked up to my friend, gave her a cuddle and said, 'This is beyond fucked. I love you and we're here for you in any way you need us to be'. At that moment, she pulled me into the hug even tighter and we just stood there for about 30 seconds in silence. It's messy and horrible but the capacity to sit with discomfort allows you to choose and exhibit more functional behaviours.

> **Trying to avoid discomfort can lead us to doing very dysfunctional things that, while good intentioned, do not serve the situation.**

Discomfort's relationship to violence

One organisation I've done a lot of work for over the years is the White Ribbon foundation. Its sole focus was to eradicate violence against women perpetrated by men. I've spoken at many public events for them over the years and also have worked with their leadership team. It was a great organisation and one with a cause very close to my heart.

At an event, I was talking to a researcher who looks at the area of violence. He said,

> Our biggest challenge is not awareness. It's very rare for a man not to know that violence against women is not okay. One of our biggest challenges is when does violence occur? When they are arguing, when they are disagreeing, when the man is stressed or angry? In an attempt to make that uncomfortable feeling go away, they often lash out and make the situation end with the only tool they have in their repertoire, which is violence. One of the things we have to teach men is the ability to sit with the emotional discomfort of disagreeing or having conflict with their partner and not using violence to resolve that situation.

Fearing discomfort stops us evolving

As I've already touched on, because we have been so obsessed with only feeling positive emotions and happiness, we see negative emotion and discomfort as a bad thing or a sign that we're getting it wrong. This inability to sit with discomfort holds back people from evolution and blocks organisations from transformation.

Many organisations that I work with in our culture change work use a 360-degree feedback tool. If you are not familiar with the 360-degree process, what happens is that everyone around you gives you feedback on the impact you have on the organisation. So, for example, the people who report to you, your peers and the people you report to all fill out a survey about your impact, and you get the results anonymously. In one of the programs we were working on, we asked each of the leaders to take their feedback and have an open discussion with their teams about it. This instruction made the majority of people in the room freak out. Many said flat out, 'I'm not sharing this feedback with my team'. And I was standing there thinking, *They gave you the feedback. It's not like by you sharing the results they are going to suddenly discover something new about you!*

I kept this thought to myself and handed out the formal homework for the workshop, which was to:

- Sit and meet with your team and discuss the feedback you received.

- Thank them for the time they spent on filling out the survey.

- Ask any clarifying questions you have about your feedback; for example, if you didn't understand parts of it or if some of the feedback contradicted itself.

- Ask for guidance around what you should work on first to improve your leadership.

- Finally, check in with your team once a month and ask them for feedback on your progress in the areas you have chosen to work on. (In effect, this last step is about their teams coaching them around their own development.)

Of course, as with any voluntary process, some leaders completed the homework and some leaders didn't.

We then studied the impact of doing or not doing the prescribed behaviours. Team members who had a leader who did the behaviours said it had an incredibly positive impact on the team culture. The teams admired the leader's bravery and vulnerability in having the conversation. Also the leader saying thank you for taking the time to fill out the survey showed genuine appreciation and also validated the importance of giving feedback. In addition, involving the team in their own leadership development built trust and connection and allowed them to have some real authentic conversations.

We also interviewed the teams whose leader didn't go back and do the five desired behaviours. Their response was along the lines of, 'What was the point of even filling out the feedback? They didn't even acknowledge the fact that it had happened. My leader never changes'. When we spoke to leaders about this activity, the block to doing it was that they couldn't sit with the discomfort of having that conversation. The discomfort made them run a mile, even though the results and payback were staggering.

The avoidance of discomfort and struggle holds back organisations on multiple fronts. I was having a conversation with one of the head analysts at a global professional services firm, and I asked him what he saw as the biggest problem in business today. Without even hesitating, he said, 'Leaders don't get bad news'. Because people don't want to have uncomfortable conversations, they cover up their mistakes. This does two things. Number one, a small mistake (which might not have had a huge impact) is covered and accumulates with other mistakes and they build on each other and then we have a disaster. Secondly, leaders never really get to know what is going on. The analyst I spoke to said one of the most effective leaders he saw regularly sat down with people and asked them 'What don't I know, that I should know about?'

Increasing comfort and declining resilience

Research professor Dr Peter Gray was invited by counselling services at a university in the United States to discuss the dramatic decline in resilience among college students. He then published his observations in September 2015 in a brilliant *Psychology Today* article titled 'Declining student resilience: A serious problem for colleges'. The article highlights that emergency calls to college counselling services had more than doubled in the last five years. However, all too often the 'crises' students were seeking help for were really just everyday problems. Two students had attended counselling because they had seen a mouse in their apartment. They had also called the police about the same issue.

He points out that facility staff have observed the following changes in students:

- Getting a bad grade crushes them and often leads to an emotional crisis.

- They see a bad grade as a reason to complain rather than a reason to study harder.

- They don't want to take risks or try new things in case they fail.

- Students expect the university to hold their hand and do everything for them.

- Universities are being asking to lower their academic standards and not challenge the students too much.

Dr Gray's work has also seen him outline the decline in younger children's chances to play and explore, and do things away from the supervision of their parents and carers. And he argues this has led to increases in anxiety and depression. In the article, he says we now have a generation of young people who don't know how to solve problems for themselves, because they haven't been given the opportunity. As he highlights,

> They have not been given the opportunity to get into trouble and find their own way out, to experience failure and realize they can survive it, to be called bad names by others and learn how to respond without adult intervention.

These kids are now young adults but, Dr Gray says, being raised this way means they find it difficult to take responsibility for their own actions and still expect someone else to solve their problems.

And don't think this only relates to US kids—we are not immune to this in my home country of Australia, either. Henrietta Cook's *Sydney Morning Herald* article 'The rise of the helicopter parent at Australian universities' from 2019 details how facility staff are reporting greater levels of interference from parents. Parents are turning up unannounced to lecturers' offices, for example, wanting to discuss their children's grades, or repeatedly phoning them to ensure that their child is progressing at the acceptable rate. One parent threatened legal action after her child missed out on a place in a tutorial because it was full. A lecturer quoted in this article said, 'In the past, students would come to complain about their mark. Now the parents come to complain about the mark'. When I attended university in the mid-1990s I would have been stunned if my parents knew the name of my course, let alone who my lecturer was. In fact, any of the people I went to university with would have been mortified if their parents set foot on campus. University was the one thing our parents didn't interfere in. This clearly no longer applies.

This point was also backed up in a conversation I recently had with a friend who is a lecturer at a university. She disclosed to me that she had been openly told she couldn't fail students—particularly international students who had paid exorbitant fees to get their degrees. Education has become a transaction, it seems, and is no longer solely about learning.

The factors that contribute to these students having a poor relationship with struggle are many and complex. I'm not blaming the students here; they are a product of a new society. What this research shows us is that protecting people from struggle and challenge ultimately does more harm than good. As a society, we are becoming increasingly comfortable—to the point where we have a lower and lower tolerance for discomfort.

My child couldn't be anything but perfect

Part of my research work is a project called 'The Flourish Movement', where I work with school leaders around their mental health and wellbeing. I've come to know the members of this group very well and some of them are now close friends. They tell me similar stories about parents being unwilling to allow their child to experience discomfort, or to sit in discomfort themselves.

One of the things they told me that has changed about the job is the inability of parents to consider that their child may be wrong or may have done something wrong. Instead, most parents come into meetings with a combative mindset and look to attack and blame. The moment it is suggested that their child has done something wrong, their response is to attack. Rather than sit with the discomfort and have a rational conversation, they accuse and attack others. The reason they act this way is that the attack makes the discomfort go away.

Think about romantic couples having an argument. Now, unfortunately, I've had some experience in this area and so know that usually when two people in a relationship are arguing it starts along the lines of, 'You do this, it drives me nuts, stop doing it, do this instead'. Now to have a constructive response in this situation, you must be able to sit with the discomfort of being wrong, the discomfort of upsetting someone and the discomfort that you will have to change. However, how does the average person respond to that dialogue? Do they say 'Oh my gosh, hun. This is such useful feedback. What else can I do to make this relationship better?' No, the average person doesn't say that. The average person says, 'Well, if I do that, you do this, and the other day you said this to me, and if your mum wouldn't get so involved in this relationship we'd be fine'.

Most people's response to feedback and criticism is to attack and make the other person feel bad and be wrong because it makes the discomfort go away. And while this might remove the discomfort in the moment, it leaves a trail of destruction and harms the relationship.

What are you most proud of?

To explore further why we don't want our life to be easy, let's shift modes. Welcome to the interactive part of the book.

Take a moment to pause, be quiet and reflect on the following question: What is the one thing you are most proud of in your whole entire life? What is it that you would hang your hat on?

STOP!

Before you start, I have some rules. Rule number one: if you have kids you can't use your kids as an example. Why? Because you just outsourced the activity to your kids. Whatever you come up with it must be about you—something you have achieved or you're proud of about yourself. Rule number two: if you are planning on discussing this with other people, make sure whatever you come up with is socially acceptable.

Have you got your example? Good!

Now, did you come up with something hard or did you come up with something easy? I bet it was something hard. Since 2013 in my keynote presentations, I have been asking this question to groups. I've now asked over 200 000 people all over the world. The most common things people are most proud of are:

- I moved countries and built a life for myself.

- I completed my degree while working full-time and having a family.

- I had the courage to change careers.

- I overcame a challenging personal situation.

- I left a dysfunctional relationship.

- I took on difficult and scary challenges in my work.

What's the common theme here? When you ask people what they're proud of, they talk about the hardest and most challenging things they've ever done. In one workshop in Europe, a woman responded by talking about the time she was kidnapped. She said, 'They abducted me and put me in a car and drove away. I was obviously terrified but I decided to fight. When they pulled up at a traffic light, I elbowed one of my abductors in the face and fled the car to safety. I was proud of the fact that I had the courage to do something about my situation rather than shrink away.

> **When you ask people what they're proud of, they talk about the hardest and most challenging things they've ever done.**

Yeah, no-one shared after that one. She had everyone beat.

By far the most hilarious one was when I was presenting to a banana growers association. I had 400 farmers in a room, all men and no women. I asked them the 'proud of' question and they started discussing it in pairs. I approached a guy in the front row who was sitting by himself. I asked him for his answer. He thought for a moment then said, 'Married my wife'.

I replied, 'No offence, but people get married every day. Why are you proud of that?'

'You haven't seen my wife,' he said. I was confused and told him so. He looked at me and said, 'Mate, I am punching so far above my weight'.

As you can see, what informs our self-esteem and self-worth are the challenging times that require us to strive and push through struggle. No-one was ever proud of the easy things! No-one in response to this question has ever put up their hand up and said, 'I watch TV like a legend! I can lie there for hours and not even move!' Nor has anyone ever said, 'I've resisted cultural change for seven years. Values? Don't know what they are'.

When we are asked what we are most proud of, we talk about the stuff that requires us to get in the trenches with struggle and fight

> **No-one was ever proud of the easy things!**

it out. Then when we crawl out the other side, we look back and think, *That's what I'm proud of.*

This even applies to organisations. A client I love to work with is an organisation called QUU, a water company in Brisbane. I was running a workshop with the senior leaders and I asked what they were proud of as an organisation. Unanimously, they all said the 2011 Brisbane floods. This was the most challenging situation they had faced as an organisation, yet they were proud of the tenacity and resilience shown by everyone. People didn't worry about titles or job descriptions; they simply rolled up their sleeves and got the job done. Even though it was an incredibly challenging and difficult time, and they wouldn't choose to go through it again, everyone agreed that it brought the organisation closer together. Many people even commented that the cultural afterglow lasted for months afterwards.

We need the hard stuff in life because it informs our self-esteem and self-worth.

What these examples tell us is that embracing and living through the struggle is the whole point. Further support of this is how we don't respect people who have had it easy. A few years back, I had arrived in Singapore, checked into my hotel room and put on the TV while I was unpacking my bag. It was when Donald Trump first ran for president. I can't remember if it was the Democratic or Republican nomination debate but what I remember is five to six people standing on stage all arguing they'd had a harder life than the others. Stories of challenging childhoods, impoverished backgrounds and difficult challenges overcome were wielded by the candidates like swords as they tried to cut down their opponents. It actually started to get humorous as each candidate claimed more and more disadvantage. The scene reminded me of the famous skit 'The Four Yorkshiremen', from *At Last the 1948 Show* in 1967 starring Tim Brooke-Taylor, John Cleese, Graham Chapman, and Marty Feldman. The sketch sees the four of them trying to outdo each other with stories of their impoverished childhood. The conversation keeps escalating—with each story ending with someone else crying 'Luxury!' before launching into their own story—until they get to the point where

John Cleese's character claims that he had to get up 'half an hour before we'd gone to bed, eat a lump of poison, work 29 hours a day at mill', to then come home and each night have their father strangle them and dance about on their graves.

You don't want things to be easy. You want them to be challenging. You want to get in the trenches with challenge and fight it out. Because when it's given to you on a platter it's devastatingly bad.

Rich kids and welfare kids are the same

In the research of this book, I interviewed a number of lawyers who work with huge family trusts. A trust is basically a pot of money (usually invested in something) that is used to support the beneficiary of the trust (the person who gets the money). Every trust has specific rules. For example, it may be that each year the beneficiary gets 50 per cent of the income that has come from the trust. Or children can only access the trust after their 25th birthday. I also interviewed welfare workers who had a long career in this area.

The trust lawyers and welfare workers are some of the most fascinating people I have ever spoken to. They have such a unique insight into human behaviour. The key message they all talked about is when people are given money that they don't have to earn or work for in some way, it is disastrous for that person. One of the lawyers said, 'I have learned there is very little difference between rich kids and welfare kids. The big difference is how expensive the drugs they take are. When a person is given money (either through welfare or their parents) without any expectations that they must do something to receive that privilege, their life goes off the rails. The life of someone who is on welfare and not doing anything to challenge or better themselves is hauntingly similar to a rich, indulged, privileged

> When a person is given money (either through welfare or their parents) without any expectations that they must do something to receive that privilege, their life goes off the rails.

person'. The most common behaviours they saw from people who got handouts and didn't have to work for them were apathy and a lack of desire to do anything, even get out of bed in the morning, drug addiction, excessive alcohol consumption, zoning out in front of screens, depression, poor self-worth, risky behaviours and partying hard. Both groups are operating in a false economy. In other words, they held the belief, 'it doesn't matter what I do because the risk is low, I have nothing to lose'.

One lawyer who had worked with incredibly wealthy families said,

> Third-generation rich kids are usually a disaster because they haven't had to earn it. They don't know what it is like to work hard and stretch themselves. It was handed to them. The first generation come from nothing and work hard to build their wealth. The first generation instil in their children (the second generation) this work ethic so the success of the family continues. Then comes the third generation and the work ethic, the hunger to achieve something and the functional relationships with challenge is lost. As a result, the wheels fall off the family business.

The family trust lawyers all said that the most functional and successful (mega) wealthy families had high expectations for their children to contribute and strive to make a difference to something bigger than themselves. One of the lawyers cited the Myer family as managing this issue really well and having created a family ethos of striving and giving back to the community.

As billionaire investor Warren Buffett famously said,

> Leave your children enough money so that they would feel they could do anything, but not so much that they could do nothing.

Further evidence for the importance of striving is the fact that the successful programs that work with disadvantaged youth have one thing in common. They help the kids to strive. They get them involved in an activity that is challenging, something that requires effort, tenacity and resilience. When they see themselves conquer something challenging and difficult, and they have had to grow and evolve to get there, their self-esteem starts to build.

The consistent thread that went through all these conversations is that for all groups, low expectations and not being challenged to evolve leads to dysfunction.

The comfort of the rich and famous

You see these same issues with celebrities and the rich as well. Having people pander to every desire and need as well as having a cast of thousands to do everything for them messes with their heads. When we become too entitled and pandered, our sense of self and self-image distorts, resulting in misery and poor behaviour.

After I finished my PhD and while I was building my research, consulting and speaking business, I paid the rent by being a personal trainer in the eastern suburbs of Sydney. I worked for John Tilden, a wonderful man whose support helped my career be where it is today. Two experiences stood out to me from this time. We used to train what people referred to as the 'eastern suburbs housewives'. This was pre-Instagram, but if social media was around back then, they would have ruled it. Why? Because on paper (or on screen) their lives were perfect. They were gorgeous and rich, with beautiful possessions, went to all the right parties and were well known in the celebrity circles. However, under this perfect surface, many of them were deeply, deeply unfulfilled.

I don't know what it is about being a personal trainer but people tell you things that they wouldn't tell anyone else. Deeply personal things. I'm not sure if it's the endorphins or the activewear, but I've been shocked more than once in a session by clients over-sharing with me. And sooner or later many of those eastern suburbs housewives broke down in tears talking about how empty their lives felt. One woman, who was the queen of the eastern suburbs set, talked about her father being a cardiothoracic surgeon who had saved countless people's lives. She sobbed as her blonde hair covered her face and she said, 'I have done nothing with my life. I haven't achieved anything. I haven't made a difference to anyone else and my life has no meaning'.

My initial thought was, *I'm not getting paid enough for this.* My second thought was these women all faced the same problem. They all had won the genetic lottery—they were stunningly good-looking and were born into wealthy, influential families. As a result, they married rich, influential men and their world was about enjoying the good life of parties, shopping, lunch, tennis, more parties and more shopping. They were high on status and pleasure but low on struggle, challenge and evolution, and they paid the price for it. In contrast to this, the 'eastern suburbs housewives' who had a fulfilling life had clear passions that contributed to others.

The second experience that stood out from my personal training days was getting to work with Guy Sebastian, the first winner of reality show *Australian Idol*. First of all, Guy is one of the nicest human beings to ever walk upright. He is supremely talented but incredibly grounded. I was training him when he was about to embark on a songwriting tour in the United States and he was extremely excited about the fact that he was going to collaborate with so many of his heroes. However, when he came back from the trip, he was incredibly dejected—because so many of his heroes had disappointed him on a personal level. He was disappointed in how they treated people, their substance abuse, their infidelity with their romantic partners as well as their attitude that they could do and get away with anything they wanted. He did talk about one musician who he loved working with. This guy was the son of a very famous sitcom actor. His dad was such an A-grade celebrity that if you dropped his name, it would open doors. However, this young musician refused to leverage his dad's fame. Instead, he changed his name, moved out of the family castle into a one-bedroom apartment, got in the trenches and earned his own success. He committed himself to song writing, playing the clubs and earning his stripes. Guy said this action made him not only a better musician but also a better human being.

Speaking of music: the majority of bands and musical acts can never replicate the success of their first one or two albums. Why? Because these albums were written when they were deep in the strive, when they were in the trenches fighting for their careers, and when they had hunger and desire. But when they have a hit album and become famous, the struggle goes away and the world starts to cater to their every whim and desire. They are no longer striving because they have made it and, as a result, their performance suffers.

The scourge of boredom

When we are no longer striving, we naturally fall into complacency and boredom. What I and my team are discovering in our research is that this is a devastating state for human beings. When I say 'boredom' I don't mean moments of boredom. Moments of boredom are fine—in fact, they are very healthy. I mean chronic boredom where you are doing the same thing, day in and day out—in other words, cruising along without struggle and challenge.

Boredom leads to dysfunction. Let me give you an example. Put two kids in the back of a car and start to drive. What do you hear after an hour? 'Are we there yet, are we there yet?' Half an hour later, they move onto fighting: 'He's on my side, she's touching me, tell him to give it back'. My favourite is, 'He's looking out my window'. Why do they fight? Because they are bored.

Look at any piece of HR research and it'll show you that bored employees are dangerous. They spread gossip, they create trouble, and they talk about people behind their back. Why? Because they are bored. And, as a result, they are looking for drama and interest. Employees who are striving to evolve and grow don't have time for that nonsense. They are too busy being immersed in the challenge.

Another example of the devastating impact of boredom is what happens to a group of youths who lack striving and instead are immersed in boredom. We all know how this tale ends: they find themselves displaying antisocial behaviours and getting into trouble with the law. Many rural towns are crippled by this, because kids in these small towns lack stimulation and an opportunity for striving. As a result, some descend into dysfunctional criminal behaviours.

THE BOREDOM OF LIVING IN LUXURY

An interesting group we studied were the expatriate, or expat, community (people residing in a country other than their native country). The following is a piece written by Aimee Chan, a writer, magazine editor and content creator who has been published in *CNN*, *Harper's BAZAAR*, *ELLE*, *Cosmopolitan*, *The Weekend Australian* and *The Straits Times*. Most importantly, she lived as an expat in Singapore for nearly ten years. Here are her perspectives on what the expat lifestyle is like.

To an outsider, being wealthy and privileged seemingly gives you very little to complain about. You have social and economic power. You can afford to delegate all the tedious tasks you don't want to do. And you are never worried about how to pay for your next meal or your children's education.

For many, this is the lure of expatriate life. Expats work in high-powered and respected jobs earning huge salaries. On top of the (apparently) excessive pay cheques, their companies also pay for their housing rental, cars, utilities, expensive international private school fees and often an additional cost of living allowance.

I was an expat for nearly ten years and it was a lavish lifestyle. Everyone around me had a live-in maid to babysit, do the laundry and cook the meals. All the kids went to school with the children of diplomats and CEOs. And a weekend away was jet-setting off to a boutique hotel in a developing country where your spending power was even more disproportionately extreme.

The impact of all this privilege and money could sometimes be surprisingly negative. The sense of community among expats was often lost (and not just because people left to go to their next expat assignment every few years). If you were sick, no-one dropped off homemade soup or offered to babysit your children. It wasn't because they weren't thinking of you — it was because everyone assumed your maid would do that. Many friendships could feel disappointingly superficial and transient.

The reliance on hired help and cheap labour in expat societies is both a luxury and a handicap. While it is enjoyable not to have to clean the toilet and to have your meals cooked to order all for a token cost, it does mean those daily tedious tasks become disproportionately hard. This is particularly obvious when expats are placed back in their home environment. Sometimes the culture shock of becoming normal again (as opposed to living as one of society's most elite) can be confusing.

Long-term expats back in Australia complain about waiting for long periods in the car at the service station, only to eventually realise that they have to get out of the car and put the petrol in themselves. Or of being told off by the checkout lady at the supermarket for handing over their credit card to pay instead of doing the swiping themselves.

The cultural gap between normal expat life and normal life in Australia can significantly affect relationships, even with family and friends back home that you see infrequently. Any expat taking a holiday back to Australia knows that it can often be cheaper and more convenient to bring your maid with you than to try to find and hire a by-the-hour babysitter. But the social backlash and judgement you will receive may not be worth the economic savings.

Adjusting to life in Australia can be so hard that many expats return only for a couple of years before deciding to backtrack and take another expat assignment elsewhere.

Familial relationships can become particularly warped in expat societies. Children don't see their parents do laundry or clean dishes. As a result, many expat kids don't have to learn how to do any menial chores on their own. While preschools in Australia encourage school readiness by requiring children to bring their own lunchboxes and hang their own bags, in many expat countries school readiness only equates with academic results. So while the children may be fluent in multiple languages and able to recite times tables, they also expect their teachers to shower them and dress them before the preschool day is over so the parents don't have to do it when they get home.

Expat marriages can be highly susceptible to strain because with extreme money comes an extreme power imbalance. One partner (often the husband) is in a highly acclaimed career with a huge earnings potential. The family enters the country on his visa. This means that the other spouse (often the wife, also known as the 'trailing spouse') becomes reliant on him for everything. Depending on the country, she usually has no legal rights and cannot be employed, open a bank account, rent a property or even own her own mobile phone number.

It is quite common for trailing spouses to experience a sense of loss, displacement and depression as an expatriate. With no work to keep them mentally stimulated and no household to run (because there is a maid), life frequently becomes about long alcohol-fuelled ladies' lunches and planning the next expensive family holiday.

The party-hard lifestyle goes hand in hand with being an expatriate. At first, the meals and parties and holidays are extravagant just because of the novelty — the spending power of an expat can be completely overwhelming and sometimes you want to indulge just because you can. But eventually it also becomes a form of release. For the trailing spouse, it can be a release from the boredom of long days where your partner is away or working late, the children are at school and there is nothing to do. For the working spouse, it is a release from the golden handcuffs.

The high salaries and opulent lifestyles of the expat world mean life is full of extreme highs. You can jetset to a private villa overseas for a weekend. You consume imported seafood and French champagne at the fanciest restaurants in town. Your driver negotiates peak hour traffic so you don't have to and you fly everywhere business class. But expat life also has many extreme lows.

For the working spouse, the pressure to maintain this standard of living is enormous, especially when there is only one salary coming into the bank account. And when you are surrounded by other really motivated and successful expats all living at the top of the corporate food chain, work becomes life. You become defined by your job title, the next promotion, the next pay rise. In most countries, your salary bracket determines the kind of visa you have so that the government is literally defining you by what you earn.

This can often be a reason many expats move so frequently. Chasing the next big job allows you to chase the next high. But it also means that with every move, everyone in the family is uprooting and starting all over again. And with every move, the sense of displacement and loss of community is exacerbated and the reliance on those extra luxuries that compensate (the domestic help, the bucket list travel, the top notch schools) becomes even more pronounced.

Aimee was just one of the many people I interviewed who had lived the expat lifestyle. They all said that while the expat lifestyle is not struggle free—for example, they face no family support and no close friends, and experience culture shock particularly if they move to a developing country where English is not the main language—the biggest challenge they face is not falling into the habit of enjoying the indulgent lifestyle. Also the low level of growth-centric struggle and striving for the partner (or the 'trailing spouse', as Aimee calls them) leads to boredom and a lack of stimulation. (I talk more about growth-centric struggle in chapter 6.) Once this happens, all sorts of dysfunction kicks in, such as overspending, overindulging and disconnecting from those around you.

Looking towards retirement

Contemplate this question. What is the worst decision you can make for your wellbeing and mental health? Take your time, if you like. You can even put on thinking music.

Time's up! Drum roll, please. It is ... Retire!

Retirement will kill you fast! Most people spend their whole life looking forward to being able to 'finally enjoy themselves' in retirement. This goal is so important to people that they often talk about tolerating a 'shitty job' for years to get there. However, the reality is that retirement often turns into a deep, empty chasm of despair that people fall into and can't get out of. They are often miserable and find the transition very, very difficult.

What I'm talking about here is the traditional type of retirement, where we stop work, put our feet up and simply take it easy. The evidence that people's mental and physical wellbeing greatly suffers from this type of change is compelling. The research also shows that the people who thrive in retirement are those who continue to engage in something challenging, meaningful and stimulating. In other words healthy retirement requires the person to continue to strive.

I saw this when my parents retired. The biggest thing, they said, was that they expected to have lots of energy and feel great because of the large amount of rest they were getting and the lack of stress from work. However, they found the opposite: when they stopped working, they were more tired and less energetic. After retirement they were lost, and it took them years to get comfortable with their new lives. I didn't see them return to their energetic and vibrant selves until they found stimulating and challenging endeavours to engage in.

When we retire, we remove the challenge and struggle that comes from work. Even though we may bitch and moan about work, it requires us to strive, and retirement takes that away.

Like the retiring athletes I talk about in the previous chapter, the people who do best in retirement start to strive for different things. They have passions, interests and projects that push their comfort zone and require them to show courage and evolve. My father transitioned into retirement easier than my mother because he had an extensive array of hobbies and interests that he pursues with passion. My mum didn't have this and, as a result, felt far more lost when she retired.

Retirement has parallels to unemployment. People who have been unemployed over the long term experience devastating drops in their mental health, wellbeing and self-esteem. Obviously, part of this comes from the financial strain unemployment puts on the household, as well as from the loss of identity and dignity. However, another part comes from the lack of stimulation and challenge. An element of striving is inherent in all jobs and when that is taken away, especially over the long term, we suffer.

How does Easy Street look now?

Basically, Easy Street leads to Dysfunctional Arsehole town, but it's our obsession with happiness (discussed in chapter 1) that has led to these dysfunctions. In contrast, striving is when we feel most fulfilled—and the next chapter looks at this in more detail.

The final point in this chapter, however, comes from the science fiction film *The Matrix*. If you have not seen the film, first of all, shame on you! Secondly, the premise of the story is that machines take over the world and use humans as living batteries to power the machines.

Humans are literally kept in pods (trust me, it is so much better than my description suggests). To keep the unconscious humans stimulated, their brains are connected to a software program that makes them think they are living a normal life. However, the program they are now connected to was not the first matrix. An earlier version, a paradise matrix, was also created. No-one in this matrix suffered; everyone was happy. But it was a complete failure. People died (or 'crops' as Agent Smith (a bad guy) describes them to Morpheus (a good guy) were lost). Agent Smith argues humans need misery and suffering; without it, their 'primitive cerebrum' keeps trying to wake up.

The point is that the first, paradise, Matrix was too perfect. It lacked challenge and struggle and people literally died because of it.

GOAL
VISION
ASPIRATION

THE STRIVE

FALL in LOVE with the WORK
THIS is WHERE the GOLD SITS

Welcome to
DYSFUNCTIONAL
ARSEHOLE TOWN

EASY ST

GETTING EVERYTHING
YOU WANT IS

HARMFUL
TO YOU!

Don't learn from
negative emotion

Guilty for
feeling unhappy

We run from
discomfort

OUR OBSESSION with HAPPINESS has
LED to THESE DYSFUNCTIONS

SUMMARY

- All striving involves some level of discomfort and struggle.

- We have become obsessed with being comfortable and it has perverted our relationship with discomfort and struggle so we now see them as bad.

- Because we see discomfort as bad, when it comes up, we try to make it go away. This not only stops us striving (and thus evolving), but also our attempts to make discomfort go away often lead to dysfunctional behaviours, such as aggression, violence, procrastination and hiding mistakes.

- We are proud of the things in life that scare us, make us uncomfortable and are often the hardest thing we have ever done.

- We get the most fulfilment and satisfaction from overcoming challenge because this allows us to grow and evolve.

- When things are easy, they feel like a hollow victory and are not fulfilling.

- Getting things without having to do anything to earn them messes us up.

- Retirement can be devastating for our wellbeing because it reduces the strive.

CHAPTER 4

What allows us to strive

So far I've built a case for the importance of striving. Striving is the state in which humans feel most alive and fulfilled. Striving is taking deliberate action towards a meaningful goal, vision or aspiration that requires you to be courageous and evolve in the face of the struggle that is inherit in the strive. Now let's look at how we strive and the elements required.

> Striving is taking deliberate action towards a meaningful goal, vision or aspiration that requires you to be courageous and evolve in the face of the struggle that is inherit in the strive.

The most fulfilling part of the striving process for the people in our research was when they overcame the struggle that inevitably came up during the strive. It makes sense, doesn't it? If we are going to strive and achieve something or stand for something, that will come with a shit tonne of struggle. Whenever you strive, there will always be struggle. Struggle is inherent in any type of growth. However, don't worry because this little cloud has a very silver lining. Overcoming struggle feels really, really, really good. And it is so satisfying because it requires us to display courage and to evolve (meaning develop new skills and capacity) into a better version of yourself in order to fulfil the strive.

> **Striving = courage + evolution**

The two elements of striving—courage and evolution—are critically important. First, let's look at courage.

The benefit of being courageous

If you were to ask the average person in the street what they wanted from life, what do you think would be the most common answer? If you guessed, 'I just want to be happy', you are right. When faced with the biggest question in life, people pull out the happiness card. Similarly, if you ask the average parent what they want for their children you get a similar response. 'I don't care. I just want them to be happy.' When people look forward in their life to what they want for themselves or for the people who mean the most to them, happiness is the focus and the objective.

I was contemplating this finding when I was struck by the thought: Looking forward in our life the objective is happiness, but is it the same for people when they look back on their life? At the end of our lives, do we reflect and think, *I wish I'd had more happiness!* To answer this question, I started to explore the deathbed research (yeah, cheery I know). Some slight variation exists in the research but a general theme can be seen around what people wished they'd had more of in their life—and it ain't happiness. The top three regrets of the dying are:

1. I wish I'd had the courage to live the life that I wanted to live not the life that other people expected me to live.

2. I wish I'd had the courage to tell people I cared about how much they meant to me more often.

3. I wish I'd had the courage to not let fear hold me back from doing the things that scared me.

So while people looking forward into their life wish for more happiness, people at the end of their life are thinking, *Screw happiness, I wish I'd had more courage.* Witnessing yourself being courageous is one of the most fulfilling and esteem-building events you will ever experience.

Focusing on evolution lights us up

Let's look now at why evolution is so important.

It's not the achievement that we desire the most, but the evolution. When we achieve something that did not stretch us to evolve and grow, it leaves us unfulfilled. Like being courageous, one of the most gratifying and rewarding experiences we can have is when we observe our own evolution.

In their 2011 *Harvard Business Review* article 'The power of small wins', Teresa Amabile and Steven J. Kramer presented their research showing that what motivates people at work the most is when they have a sense of progress, and they can see themselves evolving and getting better. Progress not only makes them more motivated and tenacious, but also elevates their level of joy, pride and wellbeing. Similarly, a critical factor that drives a person's engagement at work is feeling that sense of progress and seeing what they do on a daily basis having an impact. Taking the time to reflect on and celebrate progress improves the culture and connection within a team.

Progress even affects a person's perception of pressure. Recent studies have shown that teams who regularly reflected on their progress perceived the pressure they were under more favourably than teams who were not reflecting on progress. In fact, teams who were not reflecting on progress dramatically overestimated the negative impact of the pressure they were under.

This doesn't mean you have to have a massive win or experience some huge achievement. Reflecting on even a small win or any sort of progress makes a huge difference to how you feel and perform.

However, sadly we spend far too much time focusing on what we did wrong, how we could have done it better and where we are not achieving enough.

While Teresa Amabile and Steven J. Kramer used the term 'progress', I use the term 'evolution', because it is more personal and more emotional. Progress seems cold and detached and related to a specific goal, rather than being a goal in and of itself.

We are evolving our attitude

The good news is that we are seeing a shift in people's attitude towards what is success and that shift is moving towards a focus on striving. A study conducted at Strayer University (if you're an Aussie, trust me—this is its real name, not how some ocker Australian guy pronounces it) showed that people in the United States are dramatically changing their perception of what makes their life successful. In a 2014 interview on *Business Insider* Jacquelyn Smith quoted Dr Michael Plater, president of Strayer University, outlining that his research clearly showed Americans were no longer focused on their next big purchase—the car or the house—but were instead now focused on the personal journey. And this might involve personal goals or switching careers, or connecting with their family more.

Plater says one big takeaway from the study was that success today for a greater percentage of people is much more about setting personal goals and achieving them, than anything else.

> It's the feeling you get when you reach a new physical activity goal, connect with friends you haven't seen in a while, see your child succeed, ace a job interview, and many other small but incredibly significant life moments [...] that you have accomplished something bigger and better than yourself.

Once again this is further evidence as to why striving is more important than focusing on happiness if we want to feel like we have had a fulfilled life.

We are craving discomfort

My best friend, Murray, called me one Monday morning, his voice full of enthusiasm that was way beyond his normal level of perkiness. I asked him what had gotten into him. He replied, 'I did Tough Mudder on the weekend. It was the best thing ever'.

If you're not familiar with the concept, let me give you some background. Tough Mudder is an obstacle course like no other. It is usually about 20 kilometres long and covers unforgiving, steep and muddy terrain. Some of the obstacles include 'electroshock therapy', where the willing participants (or shall we call them victims) have to crawl through mud that contains a myriad of live wires that emit 10000 volts of electricity. Another is the 'Arctic enema'. As pleasant as it sounds, it's basically a pool of close to freezing icy water that you have to wade through—but they thought that was too easy so they cover part of the pool so you have to dive under the water to get to the other side. And we must not forget the 'funky monkey', where they grease a series of monkey bars over a pool of icy brown water.

Now for the average punter, this probably doesn't sound like a pleasurable way to spend your leisure time. However, the popularity of this course has exploded. As of 2016, over 3 million people have completed the event. And what's interesting is that people aren't just doing the challenge once, ticking off their bucket list and then never going back. People are doing multiple races every year.

Tough Mudder is not the only business of its kind, and these sorts of obstacle course races are becoming more and more popular. So what is driving this global phenomenon? Well, back to Murray.

When I asked him what made him do it, he replied, 'I was craving a challenge, I wanted something that made me feel scared and uncomfortable. Sometimes I feel that life gets a little mundane and predictable. I just had to do something that got me out of that rut. Also, I wanted to see if I could handle it and not give up'. That is it folks. There you have it, from the mouth of babes (actually from the mouth of a rather large, muscular, red-headed, hot-tempered guy). People are crying out for a challenge, and for opportunities to display courage and evolve, because they need to feel alive, they need to feel pushed, and they are tired of their sanitised world where things are mundane and safe.

The desire to strive has even transformed the fitness industry. Up until recently, if you wanted to market any fitness equipment or weight loss strategy, the following words were critical:

- easy
- simple
- little effort
- comfortable
- quick results.

Since the beginning of time it seems marketing in the fitness and weight loss industry has been about fooling people into thinking that your strategy will require no effort and deliver remarkable results. And, of course, it will all be achieved in 12 weeks (the magical number in the fitness and weight loss industry). However, arguably the most successful fitness franchise in the past ten years has been CrossFit. CrossFit combines aspects of resistance training, gymnastics, Olympic-level weightlifting and cardiovascular exercise. It is very challenging and not something you can just coast through. I have done a number of CrossFit workouts, and easy, simple and comfortable were the furthest words from my mind. The big question is how CrossFit has been so successful when it goes completely against the usual formula of the fitness industry.

One of the key drivers of its success is that participants measure progression on multiple levels. In CrossFit, you measure not only the weight lifted and number of reps, but also the time it took you to complete the workout. Every workout is an opportunity to strive for greater progression. The sense of progress literally becomes addictive.

The other attraction of these extreme activities is the connection with other people. If you watch a triathlon, you'll see it is a solo activity, and possibly downright selfish. In transitions, you never see one athlete helping another, and they go out of their way to impede each other to get a slight advantage. However, at the Tough Mudder events, you literally cannot complete the course without the help of others. CrossFit is the same. The level of collegiality in this movement is breathtaking. I visited a number of 'CrossFit Boxes' (they don't call them gyms) and they all have a consistent feeling of support. People genuinely want you to improve. Even at the CrossFit Games, the pinnacle of CrossFit competition, when the leaders finish they go back and encourage the remaining competitors.

People want to strive to get better, but they don't want to do it at the expense of other people. They want to celebrate that victory with others, and have people bear witness to their own growth and evolution, rather than sourcing self-esteem by leaving other people behind. If they have done their best and been beaten, they are respectful to those who have simply done better than them.

> People want to strive to get better, but they don't want to do it at the expense of other people. They want to celebrate that victory with others, and have people bear witness to their own growth and evolution.

I mention Mike Pagan, who supports elite sportspeople and business professionals, in chapter 2. In my interview with him, he agreed with the notion that people today are craving challenge and discomfort to prove that they are still alive, and that he has fallen victim to this as well. He recently swam the English Channel in a relay team. 'I needed to do something that scared the hell out of me. What was interesting is what I loved the most about the process was not the completion but the training and comradery with my team mates.' There you have it: striving in action.

Stress zone or strive zone?

In 2006, psychologists Andy Ryan and Dawn Markova developed a model, now used by many trainers, of three pressure zones people can inhabit. The first zone is your comfort zone. This is where you feel safe and comfortable. You don't feel distress or fear here, but you also don't experience any growth. The next layer is the stretch zone, where you take on things that stretch your skill and capability. A lot of growth occurs in this zone because you are doing things that are slightly outside your capability. The final layer is the strain or stress zone. In this zone, you experience all sorts of negative emotions such as panic and fear. This outer zone is seen as tasks that are outside your capacity. I've seen many representations of the model, but the following figure sums up the basic ideas.

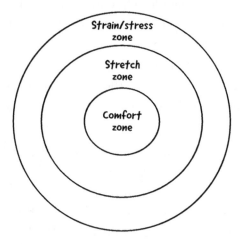

The different variations of this model say that you should stay out of the stress or strain zone because the fear and challenge is too great and you simply cannot function or learn from this phase. Instead, you should spend your time moving between the two central phases—so from your comfort zone to the stretch zone and then back to your comfort zone. The stretch zone challenges you enough so that you grow but not enough that you feel out of your depth. The findings from my research fly in the face of this model. Where most trainers, presenters or consultants say stay away from the stress zone, I say feel free to go into that zone with all guns a-blazing. This zone is where the gold is, and it is the space that really tests you and allows you to be courageous. Obviously, you don't want to spend too much time there. But don't be afraid to embrace it. Rather than just moving between the two inner zones, having a complete and fulfilled life means moving between all three zones, as shown in the following reworking of the model. Think of it as emotional interval training.

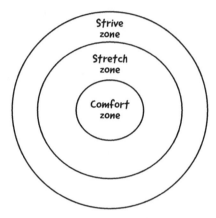

Striving improves the quality of our goals

If you look at goal-setting theory, goals can be arranged on a continuum from intrinsic to extrinsic.

Intrinsic goals satisfy our internal psychological needs to:

- grow and evolve, progress and develop a greater level of skill and mastery

- develop greater connection with others and our community, have close personal connections and be part of something bigger than us

- feel that we have some sort of control and choice around our behaviour and what we are pursuing, that these choices are informed by our values and the vision of the person we want to become and we are not acting in a way that is not coerced or influenced by others.

These types of goals are considered to be inherently rewarding to pursue, presumably because they satisfy our deep internal psychological needs directly. You pursue these goals for the sake of doing them; you are not doing them to achieve a specific outcome.

Examples of intrinsic goals are:

- be a more engaged parent and develop a loving, non-judgemental connection with my children
- be a leader who creates an environment of safety where people believe it is okay to speak up and be themselves at work
- learn a musical instrument and play in a band
- join a community group that works on a project to clean up the green spaces in the local area to encourage people to spend time in them and develop connections with other people
- work on my productivity at work and be more selective about where I spend my time so I get to the important activities
- work with a psychologist to be more accepting of myself
- enrol in a course to learn more about the subject because I find it fascinating
- exercise to have more energy and feel better.

Extrinsic goals focus on achieving an external outcome. This external reward may be praise from someone or a group, financial success, physical attractiveness, a job promotion, fame or a possession.

The focus of extrinsic goals is the triumph: the arrival and the achievement are the objectives, not the process for arriving.

Examples of extrinsic goals are:

- lose weight so I can get a romantic partner or post pictures of myself looking good on Instagram to get praise from others
- get a promotion so I can have more power and status
- learn a musical instrument and play in a band so I stand out and get more attention from people
- study hard to get into medicine so people will think I am smart
- buy a Ferrari so people will think I am successful
- study hard to get a high score
- work hard at my sport so I can win a national championship.

Extrinsic goals obviously fall into the completion myth, discussed in chapter 2. 'When I have this, then I will be [happy, worthy, loveable, fulfilled, the best ... fill in the blank here].'

A huge amount of research has demonstrated that if you are more focused on extrinsic versus intrinsic goals, you are more prone to negative outcomes. Similarly, pursuing an intrinsic goal, compared to an extrinsic goal, has been shown to be more positively correlated to physical and psychological wellbeing. Importantly, extrinsic goals aren't inherently bad. We run into trouble, however, when our focus on extrinsic goals is stronger than our focus on intrinsic goals.

Now, don't for a minute think that people who pursue extrinsic goals are shallow or bad people. Many factors, based on your culture and environment, can drive you towards extrinsic goals. These factors include:

- external threats such as poverty, war and lack of resources. The feelings of insecurity and uncertainty that stem from this can focus people on pure survival and obtaining things

- children raised by parents who are controlling and non-nurturing. As adults, these people are more likely to focus on extrinsic goals because the only time they got praise or love was when they achieved something significant or won

- work environments where you are rewarded or punished depending on whether you hit a specific set of KPIs

- controlling or dehumanising academic environments where you are only worthy if you achieve

- any environment that makes you feel like you will only be accepted if you live up to other people's standards.

However, having an extrinsic goal focus can lead to a downward spiral of cause and effect—for example, having poor relationships makes you more materialistic; being materialistic means you are less likely to focus on building quality relationships, which means you're more likely to have poor relationships.

Intrinsic motivation, on the other hand, can lead to an 'upward spiral' of wellbeing. For example, in 'Self-concordance, goal attainment, and the pursuit of happiness', Kennon Sheldon and Linda Houser-Marko found that those entering college with first-semester goals that aligned to their values and the person they wanted to become were better able to attain those goals, which then led them to feeling more comfortable and accepted at the end of that first semester. More importantly, first semester attainment also led to an even stronger setting of aligned goals for second semester, which led to more attainment and better performance during the second semester, which led to further increases in feeling that they fitted in and belonged. This striving response literally built on itself.

> **Intrinsic goals are heavily aligned to the striving process because they also focus on growth and evolution rather than the final result.**

Intrinsic goals are heavily aligned to the striving process because they also focus on growth and evolution rather than the final result. Striving (intrinsic) goals compound on themselves and drive greater success as well as better wellbeing. Intrinsic goals are focused more on personal growth and self-acceptance, affiliation and intimacy, and a sense of connection to the broader community. Such values are more likely to lead people to engage in behaviours and have experiences that are satisfying in their own right and that contribute strongly to their own growth and psychosocial development.

In contrast, extrinsic goals drive the individual towards behaviours that are not only unlikely to be enjoyable for their own sake, but can also be quite irritating and stressful (for example, working longer hours than you want to, worrying about what other people think of you and strategising about how to defeat your rivals). Perhaps you're thinking, *If extrinsic goals are not good for us, why do we live in a world where extrinsic goals seem to dominate so heavily?* Well, the answer is quite simple: it's all about threat. When people feel threatened on any level (existentially, economically or in their relationships) they run towards extrinsic goals such as financial success and status, and move away from intrinsic goals such as evolution, growth, connection with others and community contribution.

In other words, our threat response says screw self-actualisation and our ancestral drive to survive kicks in. Having resources and status is probably going to help us survive and so we move that way even though in the long term this focus takes away from our fulfilment and wellbeing. This is why people become more selfish and insular when politicians get on TV and say things like, 'Immigrants are coming to steal your jobs'. Likewise, when the media floods us with reports of a recession or economic downturn people's focus becomes, 'How do I make myself safe, even at the expense of others?'

But here's the unintended benefit of striving. The beautiful thing about the striving approach is it not only helps you leverage the most from intrinsic goals but also injects an intrinsic aspect to every extrinsic goal. The very nature of intrinsic goals is that they are about evolution and progress, and striving turns every goal into that. Striving focuses on the process and the growth and the courage and the evolution. Even if your goal is to make a million dollars a year, folding in the striving process will have you focusing on the intrinsic part of that journey. In other words, following the striving process allows you to put an intrinsic skin on any extrinsic goals, leading to higher engagement, greater performance and increased persistence.

> The beautiful thing about the striving approach is it not only helps you leverage the most from intrinsic goals but also injects an intrinsic aspect to every extrinsic goal.

What striving is not

Don't confuse striving with ambition and think that it is a purely capitalist and ego-driven concept. It is not. You can strive in your job without wanting to be the CEO. Striving is about displaying courage in the face of hard things and evolving to overcome that challenging situation. My greatest striving focus over the past two years has been in my parenting. How do I strive? To have a respectful and harmonious relationship with my daughters so that it not only fulfils us and brings us joy but also helps them evolve into the best versions of themselves. In that time I have had to be courageous to admit my mistakes, swallow my pride and apologise when I have been out of line. I have also witnessed my evolution. For example, when I have a child in front of me who is deliberately trying to push my buttons as a strategy to get what they want and be difficult on purpose, seeing myself choose constructive actions and respond to them with compassion and understanding gives me an amazing sense of evolution.

STRIVING IN BHUTAN

I once presented at a conference that included a delegation of people from Bhutan. Now Bhutan is famous for prioritising gross national happiness above gross national product. I had dinner with some of these people following the conference and I enthusiastically quizzed them about the concept. (They may say it was more like interrogation, but I call it research.) As you can probably tell from my rants about happiness earlier in this book, I went into this conversation with a lot of enthusiasm. My first question was, 'Is this the real deal or is this more of a marketing ploy for Bhutan?'

They came back very strongly, telling me this was their primary focus as a nation and every decision made at the political level was run through the lens of whether it would increase gross national happiness. They said four pillars underpin this concept:

- sustainable and equitable socio-economic development
- conservation of the environment
- preservation and promotion of culture
- good governance.

Any proposed action by the government must be filtered through these four pillars. If found to not contribute to all four, the action is rejected.

I said to them, 'Here is my problem with all this. It feels like you guys are playing small'. And I then outlined the concept of striving and made my argument for why striving was important. I said, 'It feels as

> though you are not striving; you're staying stuck'. The response was gentle but firm:
>
> This is where you are wrong. Striving makes up an essential part of our culture. We strive just as hard as Western cultures but we strive for very different things. Our exposure to Western cultures has shown us that people primarily strive for possessions and status. In Bhutan, we strive to be a great citizen, a better member of our family, to contribute more to our society and give more back to our planet. We are driven to strive just as much as people in Western cultures. We are simply striving for different things.
>
> The group from Bhutan were an excellent example of constructive striving that not only makes them better but also benefits the community and, ultimately, the planet.

One final word on what is not involved in striving. Striving is not an excuse to work yourself or others into the ground. It doesn't mean flogging yourself until you are burnt out. Perhaps you've heard the new concept of 'struggle porn'. If not, take a deep breath, it's not actual porn. Struggle porn refers to the way some people today are getting their identity and self-worth from excessive levels of struggle. They see nobility in doing crazy, unsustainable hours, living with crushing levels of stress and overcommitting themselves.

This is being driven by business writers such as Gary Vaynerchuck, who argue if you want to be successful you have to constantly hustle, be constantly working, reduce your sleep and, if you hate your job, develop a side hustle (another project in addition to your full-time job). Adding to the struggle porn message are prominent celebrities such as Dwayne 'The Rock' Johnson, who prides himself on being the hardest worker in the room. I recently saw a social media post from him that had the hashtag #teamnosleep. Of course, if you want any form of success you have to put in the hard work and earn it. But this narrative can make people think unless they are on the edge and strung out all the time, they will never make it.

In the next chapters, I talk in much more detail about embracing the struggle (and the dangers of not doing so), but let me be very clear here: we want to use the act of struggle to create growth, development and a sense of pride, not as a dysfunctional concept that drives us into the ground. As I said when discussing the comfort, stretch and strive zones, recovery from struggle is as important as getting into the trenches with it.

Embracing the struggle is also not an excuse to traumatise people with an excess of pressure. So if you're a tiger mum reading this, calm down. Striving is not pushing your kids into the deep end of the pool and saying, 'I am just helping you strive, honey'. Struggle is vitally important for people's development but it needs to be done in a supportive, nurturing way. We want to help people strive so they become a better version of themselves without driving, bullying or traumatising them. Research shows that parents who drive their children in a cold, controlling way, raise unhappy children who seek comfort in the obtainment of material possessions. (See, for example, 'The relations of maternal and social environments to late adolescents' materialistic and prosocial values' by Tim Kasser, Richard Ryan, Melvin Zax and Arnold Sameroff.)

Supporting people through struggle with empathy and understanding is an amazing opportunity to develop connection and a deep, strong bond. When we help others to be courageous and evolve, we create a bond that lasts forever.

Only you know when you are excessively dipping into struggle. Be mindful and pay attention to this.

COURAGE + EVOLUTION

THE STRIVE

WE ARE MOST FULFILLED WHEN STRIVING TOWARD a MEANINGFUL...

GOAL VISION ASPIRATION

FALL in LOVE with the WORK
THIS is WHERE the GOLD SITS

Welcome to DYSFUNCTIONAL ARSEHOLE TOWN

EASY ST

GETTING EVERYTHING YOU WANT IS

HARMFUL TO YOU!

Don't learn from negative emotion

Guilty for feeling unhappy

We run from discomfort

OUR OBSESSION with HAPPINESS has LED to THESE DYSFUNCTIONS

SUMMARY

- Striving is taking deliberate action towards a meaningful goal, vision or aspiration that requires you to be courageous and evolve in the face of the struggle that is inherent in the strive.

- Striving = courage + evolution.

- We crave to be courageous as much as we crave love, meaning and connection.

- One of our greatest regrets in life is when we retreat from the opportunity to be courageous.

- When we reflect on and witness our own evolution, it lights us up inside. We become more engaged, motivated and confident.

- Don't be afraid to step way out of your comfort zone and into the strive zone.

- The striving process helps to make all your goals more intrinsic.

- Striving is not about the accumulation of possessions or beating others.

- Striving is not an excuse to drive yourself or others into the ground; you want development, not burnout.

CHAPTER 5

The dangers of avoiding the struggle

As I mentioned in the previous chapter, if you are going to strive, you are guaranteed to run into something called struggle. I broadly define struggle as the difficulty and discomfort people experience when they are in the process of striving towards a meaningful goal, vision or aspiration.

The problem is, however, we are not wild about struggle. When you bring up the topic of people having more challenge and pressure in their lives, you rarely get an enthusiastic response. As much as we have tried to evolve, we still see pressure and challenge as something we should try to actively avoid in order to have a happy life. In a survey of over 2000 employees in Australia, my research team asked, 'Would your quality of life improve if you had less challenge and pressure?' The overwhelming majority of people said yes! But are they right? Let's explore what happens to us when we try to avoid struggle.

When I was a kid ...

It is commonplace for each generation to talk about how they had it so much harder than the youth of today. I myself have endured countless sermons from grandparents over the years about how privileged I am and that I don't fully appreciate what I have. The reality is that each generation faces its own challenges. I think it is futile to compare generations and say one had it harder than the other.

The youth of today face many challenges, such as huge levels of social comparison and harassment through social media and stagnate wage growth in many parts of the world. Soaring house prices mean, for many, home ownership is a pipe dream. Throw into the mix the huge shifts in the workforce as a result of globalisation and future shifts due to automation and artificial intelligence, and today's youth have genuine challenges that are not all in their heads.

However, a fundamental shift has occurred in the way society views and reacts to struggle, and the biggest causality of this is our youth. Let's run through those shifts.

We think discomfort and struggle will damage our children

We seem to look at our youth through a lens of them being fragile and, as a result, we have fallen into the trap of protecting the youth of today from discomfort. My research team and I interviewed a number of teachers and school principals about how parents of today parent differently from years ago. They said the main difference is that parents today will go to extraordinary lengths to stop their children feeling any sort of discomfort.

No doubt you've heard of 'helicopter parents', but they refer to them as 'lawnmower parents': they have to smooth out the path ahead for their children. What this is really doing is robbing their children of the ability to constructively deal with the real challenges they face. The lack of time spent with struggle is reducing their resilience and the size of the mental tool kit they can use when needing to deal with discomfort. As the old American proverb says, we should,

Prepare the child for the road, not the road for the child.

We've never really had to struggle and do without

While most of us in the developed world experience some challenges, we are unlikely to have had huge sweeping challenges be imposed on us. The majority of people in the West today have not experienced the impact of war. Indeed, the only wars they know about have been fought in far-off lands and they have not directly affected their lives.

The level of prosperity we are surrounded by is also staggering. My parents had to pay off their house when interest rates were at 18 per cent. They had to do without and rarely got the things they wanted. Most people have not known genuinely hard times. I saw this during the GFC in 2008. I watched an entire generation of managers who had never had to manage people in the hard times. They literally didn't know what to do.

Fortunately, in Australia, those hard times did not last long and we returned to prosperity as usual. But this is not without its ill effects as well. This is having profound impacts on our children, and I recently experienced this in my home. In contrast to me (I took my first plane trip when I was 22 years old), my eldest daughter has flown a lot because my wife is from Melbourne and, as a result, we visit her family. One morning, we had an early morning flight to Melbourne. As we were getting ready to leave for the airport, I asked my eldest daughter, who was five at the time, whether she wanted to have breakfast before we left—to which she replied, 'Nah, it's okay, Dad. I'll eat in the Qantas lounge'. It was at that point that I was struck by my children's insane levels of privilege compared to my own upbringing.

We don't have to wait for anything we want

Today, very few people have any sense of delayed gratification. If we want entertainment, we simply fire up the phone. If we want to see a movie, we just stream it straight to our TV. If we want to find a date, we just pull out the Tinder app. If we want to buy something, forget about saving up and doing without, we simply access the many forms of credit that are at our finger tips.

When I was a child we had something called 'lay-by', which at the time I thought was some sort of sick psychological torture. How it worked was that you found something you wanted to buy. If you didn't have the money to buy it outright, you told the store, 'I want this thing' and, upon receiving a small deposit, they would put it out the 'back' in some sort of retail jail. What you would do then is visit the shop from time to time and make further payments until you had paid the purchase price off. At which point, the store would release your desired item from incarceration and you were free to take it home.

Over dinner with a group of friends I brought up the 'lay-by' concept. With great animation, they started to tell stories of their 'lay-by' experiences and how, by the time they got their items, they were no longer cool, in fashion or seasonably appropriate. One poor soul told how they'd had an item of clothing on lay-by that, due to an ill-timed growth spurt, no longer fitted them by the time they picked it up. Lay-by is delayed gratification on steroids and taught people that you have to do the work before you get what you want. Some stores still offer lay-by but, with options such as Zip and Afterpay (which allow you to 'buy now, pay later'), for most people it is dead as a dodo in our 'I have to have in now' society.

The perfect life looks so easy

In the past couple of years, we've seen the rise of the 'influencer' economy. With the slow death of the traditional advertising model, organisations and agencies have had to become very clever about how they entice people to buy their products. Specifically, they have turned to people who they perceive to have influence over their target group. If you don't have quinoa in your salad and smashed avocado on your toast, let me explain what an influencer is.

Say you're selling an organic juice that comes from the Himalayas. Rather than flogging it on TV, radio and print, you throw money at some knob with a man bun and a serene look on his face who has a large social media following. In return for your investment, man bun tweets his followers a picture of the juice strategically placed on his vintage dining table and thus inspires his followers to go out and buy your product.

Your typical influencer is a young person who has some sort of social currency. Usually that currency is that they are hot, cool and lead a glamorous lifestyle that their peer group covets. This is now a new career path, with top influencers being paid large sums of money to go to openings or parties or simply wear or use products. The money that influencers received back in 2013 started modestly—around a couple of hundred dollars to attend an opening or use a product. Those figures have now exploded with some influencers charging hundreds of thousands of dollars to align their brand to something.

Now, I don't want to get into an argument about whether this is right or wrong and I'm not saying that these people haven't worked hard on their brand. The challenge here is how they impact society. The reality is many of these people don't have any discernible skills. Yet, people see them living this glamorous lifestyle and being paid to travel, go to parties and shop. From the outside, it appears that these people have this amazing life without having to work for it. Thus, people in society put up their hand and say, 'Sign me up for that!'

A friend of mine speaks in schools teaching children about financial literacy, and has done so for the past 12 years. She was recently over for dinner and I asked her the biggest difference she was seeing between kids today and kids ten years ago. She said, 'I was thinking about this recently because in the early days I would ask kids what they wanted to do with their life. They always talked about occupations—I want to be a lawyer, I want to study marketing, I want to work with computers and so on. Do you know what the most common response to the question is today? Be famous! When I ask them 'famous at what ?', they say they don't care, they just want to be famous'. To support her observation we found multiple surveys that showed the most desired career path for teenagers today was social media influencer. In fact in one survey 75 per cent of teens chose influencer and only 13 per cent chose doctor or nurse.

If you want it, just manifest it

In 2006, *The Secret* was released. The focus of the book was the law of attraction, which professes that we can have anything we want through manifestation. All we have to do is ask for it, believe that we will get it and then we will receive it. The book says that our thoughts and emotions send a frequency into the universe that attracts back events and circumstances with the same frequency. For example, if we are optimistic and happy, the universe will reward us with things that make us more optimistic and happy. So if we want to be richer we simply have to ask for more money and believe that money will come to us. If we do this the universe will pick up on that frequency and rearrange circumstances so that money floods our way.

Now, if you're reading this thinking that sounds like a load of horse shit, you would be correct. However, this book was on *The New York Times* bestseller list for 146 consecutive weeks. Over 30 million copies have been sold and it has grossed over $300 million in sales. The success of this book illustrates society's desire for things to be easy. According to this book, you don't have to work hard and you don't have to put in effort. You just have to want it and it will magically arrive. If this were true, my sex life as an 18 year old would have been very different because I am certain there was nothing I thought about more.

Everyone gets a prize!

While writing this book, I was struck by a thought about something I experienced just weeks before at my daughter's fourth birthday party. We were getting ready for the party and I was trying to be useful. In an attempt to give me something to do my wife assigned me the task of running pass the parcel. With utmost confidence I said to her, 'No worries, I have got pass the parcel nailed. Consider it done'. Ten minutes later, I triumphantly returned to my wife and handed her the toy wrapped in a multitude of layers of newspaper.

As she held the parcel she asked me why it was so light. I replied, 'Well, the toy is not that heavy'.

She said, 'What do you mean the toy? There has to be lots of toys'.

I tried to put forward my case: 'Pass the parcel only has one toy, and no-one knows which layer contains the toy. The point of the game is the excitement around who will get the toy'.

My betrothed gave me that look—the one that says, 'Did you just learn to walk upright this morning?' She replied, 'Every layer of newspaper has to have a toy. Every time they take off a sheet, the kid gets the prize and you manipulate the music to ensure that every kid gets a prize'.

I passionately argued, 'That defeats the purpose of the game. If everyone wins, there is no excitement. In fact, there is no game. Why don't we just save the newspaper, put on some music and hand out some toys?' Mid-argument I googled 'pass the parcel' and found the Macquarie Dictionary's definition for the game. I victoriously announced, 'Ah ha! Pass the parcel is defined as a children's party game in which a parcel, consisting of a prize wrapped in many layers of paper, is passed around while music plays'. I emphasised, 'A prize, one prize, singular, numero uno. Not more than one prize. Victory is mine!' I thought my wife would see the error of her ways and she would join me in my quest to teach these children a valuable life lesson. Rather, I was greeted with a look of contempt and a reply of, 'You are really starting to annoy me now'. To increase my life expectancy, I relented on my cause, shut up, found a bunch of toys and did pass parcel the way my wife told me to do it.

What I didn't expect to then happen was the resulting emotional scarring—to me. During the activity, things went downhill, and fast. I followed the script and went around the group, strategically stopping the music at each child so that everyone got a prize. I started with the most needy and insecure looking ones. I thought, *What could go wrong?* Well, apparently a lot. What I didn't bargain on was that some kids didn't want to wait their turn, and started yelling at me, 'When is it my turn? I want to go next! Why do I have to wait?' It was a full-blown mutiny. One kid left the room in tears and even my own daughter turned on me. With a look that would break any father's heart she said these crippling words: 'Daddy, you are terrible at pass the parcel!'

I think it is safe to say that children today don't hear the word 'no' nearly enough and so are less equipped to handle challenge and struggle.

We bubble wrap play

Today we're even trying to limit the amount of struggle and challenge that kids experience during play. This dawned on me a number of years ago when I took my daughters to an indoor play centre. These things are an assault on our senses, with so much noise, so much activity and children losing it in every single direction. I always walk out of those places with a headache. This one particular day, it was time to go and I had a one year old under my arm but I had lost my four year old. I couldn't find her anywhere. I finally tracked her down and I said, 'Bells, we are so late. We have to go'. As I spun around to leave I looked at the scene properly and realised everything in the room was padded. The equipment was padded, the poles that hold up the equipment were padded, and netting was everywhere to stop her falling off anything. I looked down at the ground and thought it doesn't matter if she falls off stuff because the ground is also padded.

When I was a kid, our floors weren't padded. The main surface we played on was bitumen—black, rock hard and so rough it was like a metal cheese grater against your skin. Or, perhaps you remember? If half your skin was left on it somewhere in the world, you'd remember. And our monkey bars were so high that if you fell off them, you died. Our slippery dips got so hot in summer they melted your skin off. (I know—I'm waiting for someone to shout 'Luxury!')

Kids' playgrounds today are so sanitised kids no longer understand the consequence of risky behaviour.

I was once presenting at an education conference where an international education expert talked about a recent fact-finding trip he made to Finland. He'd gone to Finland because they are held in incredible esteem and seen as having one of the greatest education systems in the world. He told the story of how he visited one of the schools in Finland and happened to arrive at lunchtime. As he pulled up he was greeted by a swarm of students climbing trees out the front of the school. However, the trees also happened to be on a median strip with a busy road on either side. He was taken aback and he said to the principal, 'How can you afford to let those students do such risky behaviours?'

The principal very calmly said, 'How can we afford not to let them do such risky behaviours?'

EVOLVING PARENTING STYLES

A school principal recently shared with me their thoughts on how they have seen parents change over the years:

Parenting styles have evolved through the generations. In the 1970s and 1980s, children were given the autonomy to be kids. They learned to use their imaginations through play, climbing trees and building things with minimal supervision, and they came home when the street lights came on. Children quickly learned independence and the laws of physics: what goes up must come down. And when they got hurt, they got back up and did it all over again.

In the late 1980s and 1990s, there was a shift in parenting to focus on physical protection. This was when the 'stackhat' era commenced, with protection soon extended to elbow and knee pads. With great intent of protection, we actually created a culture of wrapping kids in cotton wool, where parents overprotected their children from any physical harm. As a result, children stopped taking risks in fear of getting 'hurt', and indirectly learned always to play it safe.

Soon after, the next generation of parenting shifted to what is known as 'helicopter parenting'. These parents were focused on emotional protection, paying extremely close attention to all their children's experiences and problems by hovering overhead, overseeing every aspect of their child's life constantly. These parents solved all problems for their child and spoke on behalf of them, thinking they knew how to best ensure their child was always 'happy'. I would also like to point out it was during this time that 'every child is a winner' became a societal expectation with unprecedented pressure for schools to recognise and acknowledge *all*, just for showing up.

Finally, we have reached the parenting style known as 'lawn mower' parents. These parents mow a beautiful straight path in life for their child, removing all obstacles, challenges and difficulties. But doing this exponentially sets the child up to fail, because life is never smooth sailing. So when these children are confronted by variables their parents cannot control (aka life) they have no strategies, problem-solving skills or resilience to cope with failure or negative experiences or emotions. And this has a knock-on effect in their ability to recover from setbacks, rejection and failure.

This is why there is a perception of entitlement exhibited by today's generation, because parents today have not only created it, but also enabled it.

What does this mean for schools and education? An unrealistic expectation for schools to provide an individualised educational response not only to teach the academic demands of the curriculum, but also to reteach and build the social and emotional needs of each child.

Core social skills such as resilience, empathy, overcoming failure and solving conflict between friends are integral lessons learned from being a child. Sadly, these essential building blocks are lacking from children's social and emotional fabric due to the parenting styles exhibited today by removing experiences where their child may face adversity or an emotion other than 'happiness'. Therefore, is it any wonder childhood anxiety and depression have increased dramatically?

The disempowerment that comes from avoiding struggle is damaging and destructive.

When we sanitise people's world so as to limit their exposure to challenge and struggle, we not only take away their opportunity to strive and evolve but also disempower them. Ultimately, the disempowerment that comes from avoiding struggle is damaging and destructive.

Don't say the F word: Failure

The other fallout of continually retreating from discomfort and struggle is that we develop a culture where we don't talk about failure and, again, this is filtering through to our children. It seems that today we only talk about their strengths and praise them constantly about how wonderful they are. I've had the opportunity of presenting at a conference with Carol Dweck; she is psychological royalty who completed pioneering research on the fixed versus growth mindset. We were talking about children when I said to her that at the end of every day I ask my daughters three questions:

1. What went well today?

2. What did you enjoy?

3. What are you looking forward to tomorrow?

After this announcement, she shot me a judgemental look. When I asked her what was wrong with those questions, she replied that I needed to put a little bit of realism in there.

She said, 'Keep doing those questions, but add in two more'. And the additional questions were:

1. 'What did you struggle with today but not give up on?' I thought, *That is a great question. How did I miss that one?*

2. 'What did you fail at today?' I looked at her and said, 'Really?' She said, 'Yes, trust me. Ask that question'.

So I went home and asked my daughters my three standard questions, which they answered. Then I asked them the struggle question, which they actually loved and they really got into. They said, 'Oh, Daddy, I had this really difficult thing to do today but I didn't give up and I kept trying'.

Then came the failure question, and that got a different response. My younger daughter wasn't wild about answering, but she did. My older daughter didn't cope at all—in fact, she refused to answer the question. You see she's a real perfectionist and when things are not 'just right' she doesn't cope. For example, she was writing my mother a birthday card once and she made a small error. In response, she tore the card up and started again.

Over the next couple of months, I persisted with the process. Every day I would ask my daughters the five questions and my older daughter still refused to answer the failure question. But I persevered, and every day I would talk about my failures and what I had gotten wrong that day. Over time, I saw her relationship with failure start to shift and she started to answer the question. In fact, her relationship with failure started to shift so much that recently I was walking up the hallway of our house as she came in the front door from school. I said, 'Bells, how was school?'

She replied, 'Awesome! Failed at four things' and gave me a high five as she walked past.

And, of course, this doesn't just apply to children. Some research I completed with my team showed that a critical skill for a team or organisation is the capacity to have open conversations around failure. When we treat failure as a no-go topic, it starts to become shameful. This kills innovation and progress because people don't want to take risks or try new things. We were doing some research with a Japanese company, for example, and we identified that one of their biggest challenges was that failure was not something talked about in the Japanese culture. If we don't acknowledge or discuss

When we treat failure as a no-go topic, it starts to become shameful. This kills innovation and progress.

failure, however, we also don't get the opportunity to learn and grow from it.

Our inability to handle discomfort and struggle has also had a devastating impact on corporate training. How most companies evaluate training is that they survey the participants to see if they enjoyed the training. Corporate learning and development has become a popularity contest. As I have explored already, the very process of learning and growing is an uncomfortable one. We must go through discomfort to find evolution. Corporate training should challenge people; it should make people uncomfortable, by challenging their assumptions and behaviour. Good training should have you questioning your approach. It should rock your world and blow your mind. You should feel a whole range of positive and negative emotions. But because training has become a popularity contest, trainers don't want to make people uncomfortable. They want a good rating and people to leave saying, 'That was fun!'

BLOWING UP THE APPLE CART

Whenever I need a cognitive slap across the face I call a mate of mine, David Lawson. Not only is David brilliant and great fun, he can cut through bullshit faster than any known human. He is an organisation development (OD) psychologist and total maverick. Some people like to upset the apple cart; he blows the freakin' thing up. The greatest lesson I learned from David is that effective training is where you give people a visceral experience in the room. He once said to me, 'Don't sit people in a room and teach them the theory of empathy. Get them to experience empathy, and then they can unpack it and understand it'. I have learned so much from David and we need more OD leaders like him. I asked him to write a piece on his views around corporate training, and here is what he had to say.

Learning the deep lessons in life is rarely easy, or fun. To truly learn something new, we often are required to release what we think we know, to see things in a new light, to adjust our mental models to adapt to what we may have learned. This experience can be one of anxiety, confusion and frustration. Letting go of what we have held to be true and adopting new ways of looking at the world requires a social and personal vulnerability that can be difficult to face in our workplaces.

When I was young there was a TV program called *The Love Boat*, and one of the characters on the show was Julie, the cruise director. Her role was to ensure that everyone on the ship was having fun, that relationships were nurtured, and that everyone enjoyed the experience.

In my work as a learning professional, I've often felt that expectations were on me to find the latest thing, to entertain everyone, and ensure that we are all having fun. Learning assessment feedback often focused on whether those participating in the session enjoyed themselves or liked the experience. Not much focus was on how much had been learned. I would frequently remind my colleagues that I am not Julie and this wasn't *The Love Boat*. If we were going to learn together, it likely won't be fun until after the learning has happened.

Increasingly, corporate learning requests aim at entertainment rather than learning, time frames are shortened, and participant enjoyment is emphasised. Large-scale events such as conference settings are the most common environments (any individual learning can be done online right?), with a largely passive audience (participants who just sit there listening). This is learning as theatre, a popularity contest with the winners being the teachers that make me feel good, not those who help me move through the anxiety and confusion that learning requires.

In fulfilling such requests, we limit ourselves in our ability to support the learning that people genuinely need — pulling our punches, becoming overly concerned with the likes, we hold back from supporting our learners to navigate the tension and discomfort that great learning often requires.

SUMMARY

- If you are going to strive, schedule in an appointment with struggle. Struggle is inherent in striving.

- Struggle is the difficulty and discomfort people experience when they are in the process of striving towards a meaningful goal, vision or aspiration.

- The big block to having a more functional relationship with struggle is we find it difficult to sit with discomfort.

- We can't evolve if we don't get in the trenches with struggle. Prioritising comfort means sacrificing courage and evolution.

- Our desire to be comfortable has got us seeing failure as a bad thing that should be avoided.

- The youth of today have been raised to believe that struggle is bad and something that should be avoided.

- Pass the parcel is a minefield of shame and humiliation that should be avoided like the plague ... or at the very least outsourced to someone else.

CHAPTER 6

The gift of struggle

Defining struggle for an individual is tricky because it is deeply personal, and different for different people. If you suffer from chronic pain, just getting out of bed may be a struggle. Struggle is also relative to context, and so is a moving challenge that varies depending on what is going on for a person. If you come from a war-torn country, your idea of what is a struggle is going to be very different from that of a latte-sipping, brunch-eating, wealthy white guy from the north shore of Sydney. (Not that I know any of them ...)

What we do know about struggle is that it has gotten a bad rap. In the previous chapter, I discussed the dangers of avoiding struggle. Here, I talk about the gifts that come from accepting struggle. A life without struggle is a life without growth. In fact, the more struggle we experience in the strive, the more satisfying it is. Our success as a species has come from our ability to embrace and overcome struggle. Struggle is a sign that we are experiencing learning and growth. Wellbeing is just not about our ability to thrive but also our ability to navigate and respond appropriately to struggle. Struggle would be less painful and less uncomfortable if we normalised it. Rather than demonising it we need to bring it out into the open, embrace it, and form a more functional relationship with it.

Understanding the four types of struggle

In my team's research and interviews, we came across four main different types of struggle. While I don't want you get too hung up on these definitions (I fully acknowledge some crossover is possible), the following sections outline what we are focusing on in our research.

Traumatic struggle

Traumatic struggle is where a person goes through a traumatic experience that has a deep and long-lasting effect on them. Very few people actually experience trauma. We have gotten pretty loose with this word and tend to attach the label to many experiences. Examples of trauma are living through war or political violence (such as civil war or terrorism, or becoming a refugee), sexual or physical abuse, experiencing a natural disaster (such as a hurricane, floods or fire), witnessing murder or extreme violence, experiencing the death of a child and extreme poverty.

Sorrowful struggle

This is struggle that results in great sadness and pain. Examples include the death of a loved one from natural causes, being injured in a car accident, a partner having an affair, being bullied at work and experiencing significant financial distress. These things really knock us around and lead to sorrow, but they are normal parts of life that people go through. Most people recover from these experiences even without the help of intervention (counselling).

The struggle in the dredge

At the other extreme to traumatic struggle, we have struggle that comes from the daily dredge of the shit we have to do that stresses us out and is not enjoyable. Examples of this are things like bad traffic, kids who won't put their shoes on so you can leave for work on time, a to-do list that is longer than your arm, getting interrupted at work so much you don't get anything done and you fall behind, having to decide what to cook for dinner, missing a flight, your manager changing their mind constantly around the focus of a project you are working on, or working in a job that you don't find stimulating or challenging. It's just stuff that frustrates you and causes stress. I hate the dredge!

We experience this sort of struggle because of some sort of gap. For example, perhaps the struggle is due to a lack of time, support, materials, autonomy, meaning, relational support or skills (you don't have the internal resources).

When we interviewed people about the importance of struggle in our lives, the most common reaction we got was along the lines of, 'The last thing I need is more struggle'. Other comments included, 'I am barely getting through the day', 'My life feels like a slog', 'I never turn off and I just feel drained', 'I am tired, I eat crap, I can't fit in exercise and I am so disconnected from my partner that I feel like we are roommates who run a very small day care centre. When people made statements like these, they were thinking about and referring to the struggle in the dredge. This struggle wears us down and takes the shine off us. The solution to this type of struggle is to add in more stuff that makes us feel alive and helps us strive.

Growth-centric struggle

The three types of struggle I've just mentioned are not the focus of this book. In terms of traumatic and sorrowful struggle and how it relates to striving, a significant body of work shows human beings can evolve and grow from the trauma that they experience. The process is incredibly difficult and often takes a special kind of person or a tremendous amount of work, but numerous case studies have shown people can come out of traumatic events stronger and more evolved because of it. They have literally strived through trauma.

Because of these three types of struggle, however, we have an avoidance or dysfunctional relationship with struggle. As already discussed in the previous chapter, we often think we need to avoid all discomfort and struggle, and now here I am saying, 'Let's embrace more struggle!' (And you're perhaps thinking, *How do I get a refund on this book?*)

However, take a breath and let me introduce you to the beauty and gifts found in a specific kind of struggle: growth-centric struggle. This struggle is the discomfort that comes in the face of challenge. It is struggle that gives you the opportunity to grow and evolve and so become a better version of yourself. It is something you could choose to avoid but if you face up to that struggle, the experience of overcoming it will lead to significant personal growth. Often, growth-centric struggle comes in the form of tasks that have low interest and low enjoyment for you. It brings discomfort for you but gives you the opportunity to exhibit courage and evolution.

> Growth-centric struggle ... gives you the opportunity to grow and evolve and so become a better version of yourself.

Growth-centric struggle is the discomfort that comes in the face of challenge. It is struggle that gives you the opportunity to grow and evolve and so become a better version of yourself.

Examples of growth-centric struggle include:

- having a hard conversation with a staff member about their behaviour
- admitting you were wrong
- getting out of bed early in the morning to exercise when it is freezing outside
- dealing with a client choosing to go with a competitor instead of you, meaning you will no longer hit budget
- dealing with losing your job
- your company going through a restructure at work and you having to report to a manager you don't like
- your company changing the technology platform you work on, and so you have to change your approach to work

- your child consistently getting in trouble at school for poor behaviour
- giving feedback to your manager about a behaviour you find inappropriate
- changing the way you run your day to be more efficient
- expressing your feelings to your partner about aspects of your relationship that you are not happy with
- addressing cultural issues in your team that you think are leading to dysfunction
- starting to take care of yourself even though you feel guilty and selfish when you do it.

In all of these examples, growth-centric struggle occurs when you meet challenge head on and drag it into the trenches and sort it out.

Let me give you some proof as to why this type of struggle is good for us.

We love leaders who push us into growth-centric struggle

Over the past five years we have interviewed, surveyed and run workshops with tens of thousands of people. One of the questions we often ask is, 'Who was your best leader and, most importantly, why?' Our data shows two standout responses to this question. Number one (by a nose) is, 'They cared about me as a person'. People said their best leader was one they knew genuinely cared about them as a human being. They made statements such as, 'They cared about my wellbeing, my career, my personal life and my family' and 'I wasn't just something that produced work. I was a person to them'.

The second response (and there was daylight after these two) was, 'They really challenged me and had high expectations of me and my work, and they held me accountable for delivering on that work'.

This one we didn't expect. Like, WTF?! Their leader gave them hard, challenging work, and held them to account for getting it done, and they loved them for that? In other words, working under their favourite leader, they had more struggle and challenge in their work. Their best leader dialled up the growth-centric struggle.

Upon further analysis, another key finding was the significant support their best leader gave them during that challenge. Some people said, 'While that leader challenged me and pushed me, they gave me support and I felt safe to try things or take risks without fear of judgement or persecution'.

Struggle makes you more engaged at work

A number of years ago, my research team and I completed a study into a group of over 1000 managers of varying levels of seniority. In the research, we found that we could classify the pressure they felt into two main types: time pressure and growth pressure. Time pressure was where they had a lot of work to do, but they had the capacity to complete it. It was not overly hard; there was just lots of it. In contrast, growth pressure was where they had a situation or challenge that was outside their skill set and reach. Or it was something where they had to dig deep and come up with ideas to complete it. It required them to bring all of themselves.

When we compared the two, growth pressure had far more struggle and challenge attached to it. On paper, the managers should not have enjoyed that type of work because of the high level of struggle. Our studies conclusively showed, however, that the most fulfilling and engaging parts of their jobs fell under the description of growth pressure. These were the moments they enjoyed their role the most, even though they often led to uncertainty and anxiety. They said they felt most engaged and alive at work when they were under growth pressure. In fact, the higher the level of challenge within this growth pressure, the greater the likelihood that they would get into flow (that highly engaged, focused state). So while time pressure was a walk in the park in terms of how hard the work was, the stretch associated with the growth pressure struggle brought out the best in them.

Struggling can help you flourish

In chapter 3, I mention the 'Flourish Movement' research project. This project, which we have been running over the past three years, is one of the greatest projects I have ever worked on. It was instigated by Bob Willetts, a terrific man and the principal of Berry Primary School in southern New South Wales, who engaged me to design and develop a program to improve the effectiveness and wellbeing of school leaders. The resulting Flourish Movement project is conducted over a 12-month period, where leaders participate in a full-day workshop each quarter, with behaviour change support provided in between workshops. A research phase also occurs at the start and the end, consisting of a 10-day diary study, interviews and a survey.

The findings of the Flourish Movement backed up our time pressure versus growth pressure finding. In the research phase, we asked the school leaders to predict how much flow they felt they had in each part of their job. We broke flow into five components, challenge, skill, enjoyment, interest and time, which they then rated individually. Because the job is such a huge vocation for them, the school leaders usually predicted their flow rates as being extremely high. However, when they filled out the diary studies of how much flow they felt in the moment, it was quite low.

Upon further analysis, we saw the reason for this was that the majority of their day is full of time pressure—specifically, meetings, admin, compliance, reporting, emails and phone calls. Due to the high level of expertise and sophistication that the school leaders possessed, these time pressure tasks did not stretch them or stimulate them in any way. As a result, we saw significant drops in mood and energy levels as the day went on. These tasks literally sucked the life out of them.

The parts of the job that gave them flow were things like leading teaching and learning, research, innovation around learning, strategy and coaching—even dealing with conflict scored higher. When we interviewed participants, they said that while those tasks were far more challenging, they were the parts of the job they loved. Those tasks were the reason they got into the job in the first place. They had meaning and purpose attached to them. Tragically, many of the school leaders are falling out of love with the job because the volume of time pressure tasks is slowly growing and cannibalising the growth-centric struggle parts of the role that pushed them and required them to evolve.

One of the focuses of the Flourish Movement became helping the school leaders spend more time in the parts of the job that they loved. The four workshops we cover are:

- How to make recovery a regular habit—preventing burnout

- Living above the chaos—getting control of your environment

- Controlling the voices—effectively dealing with negative or unhelpful thoughts and emotions

- Finding your true north—being an aligned leader.

Through having greater wellbeing, greater clarity around what they wanted to achieve, strategies that helped them use their time more effectively and clear boundaries in place, the school leaders were able to increase the time they spent in the following areas:

- strategy and planning by 28.2 per cent

- research by 39.8 per cent

- coaching of their teams by 57.1 per cent

- leading teaching and learning by 24.1 per cent

- people development by 19.5 per cent.

This meant they spent far more time in growth-centric struggle.

We also observed the following improvements:

- The principals perceived that work pressure had reduced by 18.4 per cent.

- Stress levels also reduced by 20.4 per cent and the impact of stressful issues on them dropped by 14 per cent.

- Agreement with the statements 'My life is ideal' and 'I am in good health' increased by 15 per cent and 12 per cent respectively.

- Hope increased by 11 per cent, optimism by 10 per cent and resilience by 11 per cent.

- Energy levels increased by 13.2 per cent and mood increased by 13 per cent.

Overall, greater growth-centric struggle played a role in these people becoming better versions of themselves and enjoying their life and work more. Higher levels of struggle added to their wellbeing, it didn't take away from it.

Struggling to find your mojo?

It's always slightly unsettling to see yourself reflected back in your own research. For the two years prior to writing this book, I've felt ... flat. This was confirmed to me by Linda, a friend of mine. We were having lunch and she asked how I was. I replied, 'Hmm, I'm okay, just lacking a bit of mojo'. She said, 'You've been lacking mojo for years. It's kind of like you've been stuck in neutral'. Yeah, she doesn't beat around the bush.

On my way home I reflected on our conversation and realised she was right. I had been feeling flat for quite some time. I then started to think why this was the case. On paper, things for me were great—in fact, they were better than great. I lived in a beautiful house, drove my dream car and had a job I loved. Work was great and we were completing some amazing projects. In particular, the mental health and wellbeing program with school leaders I've just talked about was not only fulfilling but was also making a real difference in their lives. My personal life was rocking too: I was married to a fabulous woman who couldn't be more wonderful, and had two beautiful children who were healthy and full of life. (They were also prone to driving me nuts, but that's what you sign up for, right?) Looking at my life, I shouldn't have been feeling flat—I should have been high-fiving people as I ran down the street.

Then it dawned on me: I was living my research. I was no longer striving. I had achieved everything I wanted and it was making me miserable. I was in cruise mode, with very little growth-centric struggle. While I wasn't miserable, I wasn't thriving. I had stopped promoting the work we were doing and the amazing findings we were getting from the research. I wasn't showcasing and sharing it with the world, and we were just existing in our little bubble. I was sitting on four book ideas but didn't have the desire to finish any of them. In fact, my publisher said that I'd set the record for procrastination around finishing a book. Then something glorious happened and struggle came back into my life with gusto.

I was working at my desk when I received an email from a client. The subject line of the email was 'This looks familiar'. It was a YouTube link to a clip where another speaker I knew from around the traps was being interviewed. As the interview went on, I started to get a sick feeling inside my stomach—I was watching one of my main keynote presentations be recited by another speaker on national TV. The keynote presentation in question relates to everything covered in this book.

I've been delivering this presentation since 2014. It has evolved and changed over the years but essentially it starts with me asking the audience to come up with the thing they are most proud of in their life. As I talk about in chapter 3, what comes out of that activity is that people begin to realise that out of the difficult and challenging things they face comes pride and self-esteem. I then ask why we give children a ribbon for coming tenth in a running race, why we can't allow anyone to lose today and why everyone has to get a prize (similar to my discussion of pass the parcel fun in chapter 5). Then I talk about how my daughter's play centre is completely padded (as I also talk about in chapter 5) and then even put up pictures of what our playgrounds were like when we were kids. Finally, I present my team's research around struggle and how out of struggle come our greatest growth and evolution.

And now I was watching this keynote speaker recite my presentation, using the exact same examples to tell the exact same story. Oh, and a bit of back story: this presenter had sat through my presentation twice. Twice he had seen me present this and sat there taking notes.

In the speaking world, you might borrow a case study, an example or even a joke from another speaker. What you don't do is copy their entire presentation. I sent the clip to a couple of clients, MCs and other presenters who had seen me do it and asked them if they saw similarities. I wanted to make sure I hadn't made up the copying and I wasn't being biased. All of them confirmed my thoughts. In fact, one of them said to me, 'If emulation is the highest form of flattery, that guy just flattered the shit out of you!'

I went onto his website to find out he'd even called his new presentation the same as mine. For a moment I thought I was being set up by my mates again and this was some sort of practical joke (similar to my initial reaction when Sheikha Intisar called). But even my mates couldn't pull off something this elaborate. So I called the other speaker straightaway but rather than being greeted with a reasonable response, I was greeted with denial, defensiveness and accusations of his own. Clearly this was going nowhere.

I spent the next couple of days being massively pissed off. I would have said at the time my predominant emotion was anger but, as I reflect on it now, I realise my predominant emotion was sadness and betrayal. I felt betrayed and a sense of injustice that I don't think I'd come across before. How can it be that you can work on something so hard and for so long and someone can come along and pass it off as their own?

Once I got over the shock of what had happened, however, I was energised beyond belief. Talk about mojo—I had it seeping out of my pores. I had struggle in front of me and I was gonna drag it into the trenches and start brawling. The following week, I cleared four days in my schedule and went away and started working on this book. I wrote an average of 10000 words each day. Back in the office, the struggle was having a similar impact on my team, and I have never seen them work so hard. They were developing marketing plans, coming up with ways to protect my IP, and working on a social media strategy. The experience had hit my team hard—after watching the video, one of my team was in tears and said, 'I don't understand how someone can just take your work'. But we as a team got into the trenches together and it bonded us. The striving to overcome this struggle was the united force that brought us together.

Now, rage and frustration can only drive you for so long and can quickly slip into dysfunction. However, it was the fuse that started our engagement and we very quickly redefined what we wanted to achieve as a business. We very quickly fell in love with the work again and that has been our driving force since.

Getting your arse kicked makes you better

As the previous story might have indicated, a big part of my work over the past 15 years has been presenting my team's research findings at various corporate conferences. In effect, I'm a professional speaker.

In that time I have delivered over 2000 presentations to more than a quarter of a million people. Some people perceive that this job is glamorous or even easy. However, I find it incredibly challenging. The travel is brutal, homesickness is heartbreaking, you can't have a sick day and the work can be draining. The struggle is real, but that is what makes it so satisfying.

I was set up to embrace the struggle right from the start. I got into speaking while I was an academic at university, when I signed up for a 'How to teach adults in a fun and exciting way' course run by a guy called Doug Malouf. Little did I know that he was one of Australia's top keynote speakers. From the start of the presentation, I was transfixed. I was in awe of this guy's mastery and capacity to engage a group. I thought I had found religion. At the morning tea break, I went up to him and said, 'I want to do what you do. Can you teach me?' He asked me how serious I was and I told him I'd never been more serious about anything in my life. I also told him I was an academic at the university and my soul was dying. He said, 'If you're serious, come to my office tomorrow [which was a Saturday] at 9 am and we will chat'.

I turned up at 8.45 am. Upon seeing me, Doug said, 'I've got a few things to do. Wait here'. At 2.30 pm, he finally came out of his office and said, 'Are you still here?' Then he told me to follow him into a training room where he pulled out a sheet of paper and said, 'Go read that to the wall'. I asked him if he was serious and his response was a very sarcastic one: 'I have never been more serious about anything in my life'. He was using my own material against me.

The passage he gave me was titled, 'The bus driver story'. It starts off with, 'You are driving a bus. At the first stop, three people get off and then four people get on ...' and it goes on and on and on. I started to read it to the wall. At the end he said, 'You talk too fast. Slow it down. Practise speaking slowly every day and come back and see me in a month'. So I did. I turned up a month later, he took me into the training room, handed me the bus driver story and told me to read it to the wall. I did. He said, 'Good. You have slowed down. But the problem now is you didn't pause. The difference between a good speaker and a bad speaker is their ability to pause. When you hit a full stop, pause for three seconds; when you hit a comma, pause for 1.5 seconds. Go home, practise it every day, see you in a month'.

I thought this guy had gone full *Karate Kid* on me. I expected the next month to paint the fence or wax his car. For the next seven months, I went through this torture, every month focusing on a different theme, different modulation in the voice or hand gestures, standing still without movement, eye contact or variety of pace. One approach he really seemed to enjoy was playing the theme to *Beverly Hills Cop* at full volume in the background while I practised. (I now have an involuntarily convulsion every time I hear that on the radio.) At the seventh month mark, I cracked it. I said, 'With all due respect, Mr Malouf, I asked you to teach me how to present to an audience and for seven months you've had me speaking to a brick wall. Is this some sort of sick joke?'

He replied, 'First of all, I had to work out if you were serious or not. Every single time I present I have people come up and say they want to be a professional speaker and they want my help. This process weeds out serious ones from the whackers [that was his favourite word]. Secondly, in seven months, you have eradicated every single mistake that the majority of professional speakers make. You are now ready for a live audience'.

Oh my God, he totally Mr Miyagied me!

And kicked around some more ...

But the struggle didn't end there.

My first presentation was beyond terrible. Let me set the scene: I had not long finished my PhD and to say I was ideological was an understatement; I thought I was gonna save the world. At the time, health and wellbeing was a big topic in the speaking world and, because part of my PhD explored wellbeing and quality of life, I thought I was well placed and qualified to address this issue. So I wrote a keynote presentation around health and wellbeing and, because I was so full of myself, I wrote a no holds barred, hit them between the eyes presentation that no-one would forget. Let me describe the first couple of minutes.

I walked out on stage and next to me was a flip chart with ten stick figures drawn on it. I turned to the audience and said, 'These ten stick figures represent everyone in this room and here is how you're going to die. Three of you will die of cancer, four will have a heart attack ...' and I kept going until they were all dead.

Now, if that wasn't bad enough, I then began to build a case around how people don't place a high enough priority on their health and wellbeing. In other words, they don't see having good health and wellbeing as being successful. Success for most people is having a nice car, a nice house, luxury holidays and getting the promotion. They don't think, *I've got good health and wellbeing—wow, I'm really successful*. To be truthful, the main strategy I was using here was to guilt and shame people into placing more importance on their health.

To drive my point home I began to talk about the bell curve of success (a model that outlines our definition of success at different ages from birth to death). The bell curve of success is a joke dressed up as a psychological model. How I delivered it was I had a bell curve on a flip chart with the numbers 3, 12, 17, 20, 30, 40, 50, 70, 75, 80,

85 drawn around the outside of the bell curve. They represented the ages we move through as we go through life. At this point, I said, 'The bell curve of success outlines our definition of success as we move through our life, and it starts when we are three. Success for us when we are three is not peeing our pants [which I wrote on the flipchart]. At 12, success is having friends because we all want to be popular at 12. At 17 success is having a driver's licence, but at 20 success is having sex. At 30 success is money, at 40 success is money and at 50 success is also having money. However, at 70 success [pause for dramatic effect] is having sex, at 75 success is having a driver's licence, at 80 success is having friends and [no doubt you are already there ... you guessed it] success at 85 is not peeing your pants.

So that was the first couple of minutes of my keynote presentation. Very subtle, I think you will agree.

But I got a booking and was asked by a Rotary Club to present to them at the Bankstown Sports Club. Not knowing what a Rotary Club was, I turned up, I had my stick figures, I had my markers and I was there to tell these people how it is. I walked in, I looked around, and to my horror everyone was over the age of 75. It was a sea of cardigans and slippers, there was barely a hair follicle in the place. I thought, *Oh God, OH GOD!!!! I only know one talk, the pee in your pants at 85 talk, and I'm talking to a bunch of old people.* I literally went to run for it, but the guy who'd booked me saw me walk in and said, 'Come on in, welcome, welcome'. I started to freak out. My main thought was focused on what would I do. Resigned to my fate, however, I thought, *Screw it. I will have to do the talk.* I did it and they hated me. Think about it: I walk in, tell them how they are going to die, which is not that far off, and that it is a miracle if they don't piss themselves by the end of my presentation. It was the longest hour of my life.

However, if I had my time over again, I wouldn't change all the screw ups, all the failures and all the struggle—because that's the stuff that builds your self-esteem and capability. Without the struggle, you don't gain the skills and victory doesn't mean as much to you when you come out the other side.

> **Without the struggle, you don't gain the skills and victory doesn't mean as much to you when you come out the other side.**

If you want to lead a full and purposeful life, don't shy away from the things that kick your arse—they make you better.

SUMMARY

- Struggle is less painful and less uncomfortable when we normalise it. Rather than demonising struggle, we need to bring it out into the open, embrace it, and form a more functional relationship with it. Embrace the gift of struggle.

- The four main types of struggle are:

    - traumatic struggle

    - sorrowful struggle

    - struggle in the dredge

    - growth-centric struggle.

- Growth-centric struggle is what comes up when you are being courageous and evolving while you are striving. It has huge benefit because it makes you more engaged and motivated at work and in life.

- Getting your arse kicked is important, and builds resilience and character.

CHAPTER 7

Making struggle your friend

I've already mentioned the ten years I've spent completing different research projects with Dr John Molineux at Deakin University. One of the things we have been exploring is what enables and drives transformation in organisations. The current business landscape requires organisations to rethink their models of operation as well as the value that they bring to their customers. Put simply, people within organisations are having to rapidly change their mindset and their behaviour to help the organisation evolve and stay relevant. As has been a theme through this book, one of the things that blocks transformation in people is their inability to sit with the discomfort that comes with struggle. Whenever you try to transform and evolve your behaviour, struggle will show up on your doorstep. What you do with that struggle will determine whether you transform or stay the same.

Struggle = development

To understand how people can have a more functional relationship with struggle and challenge, we studied 821 leaders who were leading in complex environments that were changing. We observed who of those 821 leaders was transforming and evolving their behaviour (such as improving the way they led, innovating the way their teams ran and collaborating with others to get different points of view), versus who was repeating old, safe behaviours and just doing the same old things.

One of the big differences between those two groups was their relationship with struggle. The leaders who were evolving saw the struggle associated with change as an opportunity to develop and grow. Now, they weren't weird. They didn't think, *Oh wow, I love struggle. It's so great.* No. They openly admitted how much it frightened them and how uncomfortable it was. But they had the attitude that in order to grow and evolve they had to wade through the struggle. The key behaviour they exhibited was that, when in the midst of struggle, they focused on the specific growth achieved. So if they had to lead differently, their internal dialogue was, 'How will I grow as a human being in order to handle this?', 'How will I have to evolve as a person to adapt my leadership?' If they had to change the way they interacted with customers, their mindset was, 'How do I become more masterful at active listening to really understand what is frustrating them about our service?'

The leaders who were not transforming had a very different relationship with struggle. They saw struggle as a threat. Their mindset was, 'What if I can't handle this, what if I can't evolve, what if I can't do those new behaviours, what if I can't lead that way?' And they got stuck in that narrative loop. As a result, their response to struggle was, 'How do I avoid this challenge?' or, more frequently, 'How do I blame someone else for this challenge?'

The mindset of seeing struggle as an opportunity to develop and grow as opposed to a threat was absolutely vital.

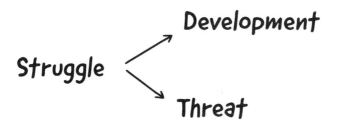

Striving response — These people sat with the discomfort long enough to evolve

Struggle → Development

Struggle → Threat

Threat response — These people retreated back to old safe behaviours

Struggle can improve our wellbeing

My team and I did other studies (with various occupations and industries) that showed that the presence of challenge and struggle was not a bad thing for people and was, in fact, correlated with better levels of wellbeing, performance, health and fulfilment, greater levels of absorption in work, increased levels of enjoyment and higher levels of intrinsic work motivation (that is, people do the work because they are enjoying the work).

However, this only occurred in individuals who had a striving response to challenge and pressure and so saw struggle and challenge as an opportunity to evolve and develop. In contrast, if the individual saw the pressure or challenge as a threat (I could screw this up, what if I can't cope? what if people think I don't know what I am doing?), it resulted in huge increases in anxiety and stress, a feeling of emotional exhaustion, greater chance of burnout, as well as a reduction in their levels of wellbeing, performance, health and fulfilment.

Embracing struggle helps us be a better leader

Working in leadership development for the past 15 years, I have seen the threat response make leaders retreat from struggle. A project that provided clear examples of this was one where we asked leaders (who had just received feedback from teams on their leadership) to do three behaviours over the following two months before the next workshop. They were:

- Sit down with their team and thank them for providing the feedback, ask any clarifying questions and ask for three things they should work on to be a better leader.

- When their team members came to them with a problem, rather than solve it for them, use a coaching process to have them come up with their own solution.

- At least every two weeks, talk to their team members about what they were doing well, how they were progressing and the positive impact that had on the team. (And this didn't have to be a formal meeting; it could just be a casual conversation.)

The reason we asked them to embrace these three behaviours is because they have been shown to dramatically improve the culture and capability of a team.

We then measured if the leaders did these behaviours through two different methods—we surveyed the leaders themselves and asked the team members if they had observed the behaviours in their leaders. We also completed a short interview with the leaders about their attitude towards the behaviours and if they were successful at implementing them. What determined if the leaders did the behaviours or not was whether they had a striving or threat response to struggle.

We saw three main groups:

- those who didn't try the behaviours at all
- those who tried them but stopped engaging quite rapidly
- those who consistently did the behaviours.

Here is what the interviews showed was going on for each of these groups.

Those who didn't try the behaviours at all

These people were in a threat state from the start, even as we outlined the behaviours during the workshop. They literally shut down and rejected the idea from the start. Excuses made later were statements such as:

- 'I was too busy to do that.'
- 'That wouldn't work for my team.'
- 'We don't have that kind of culture.'
- 'They won't respect me.'
- 'Leaders give feedback, they don't get feedback.'
- 'My team aren't good at having those conversations.'
- 'They will think I am weak and incompetent.'
- 'We are supposed to have all the answers.'
- 'I think this is a stupid exercise.'

What underpinned all these responses were fear and a belief that they were unable to evolve.

Those who tried them but stopped engaging quite rapidly

In the workshop, the leaders in this group thought it sounded like a good idea so they went out and tried the behaviours. However, because they hadn't done them before, they felt strange and so started to stress about aspects such as 'Am I doing it right?', 'Do I look stupid to my team?', 'What if I say the wrong thing?' These uncomfortable thoughts and feelings quickly put them into a threat state and so, as a result, they gave up on the new behaviours. How they framed it to me and my research team was through statements like the following:

- 'That didn't work for my team.'
- 'It made them uncomfortable.'
- 'We have a big project on so we couldn't afford the time.'

While they could see the value in doing the behaviours, these leaders could not tolerate the discomfort that came up for them.

When we explored the last group, it was a very different story.

Those who consistently did the behaviours

This group was super interesting. They obviously did the behaviours we asked them to do but what was most fascinating was how they went about doing them. The surprising finding was that this group found doing those behaviours very confronting and stressful. It wasn't as if they found them easy and that's why they were able to do them. They experienced huge levels of discomfort while doing the behaviours. As they went into the meeting with their team to ask for feedback, they were extremely nervous. Also, when they were coaching their people, they often had thoughts along the lines of, *Oh my God, am I messing this up?* and, *Do they think I'm an idiot?*

> Having this mindset of 'struggle equals development and being uncomfortable is the price you pay for evolution' had a profound impact on people's ability to sit with the struggle and evolve their behaviour.

When we asked them why they continued with these behaviours, even though they caused this large amount of stress, two main themes came out. First of all, they had a strong desire to improve and evolve as a leader. They saw that these behaviours were critical and important and would help them achieve that evolution. Secondly, they knew that if they were going to try new things and evolve a period of discomfort would occur. One leader said, 'The currency you have to pay to get better as a leader is experiencing vulnerability and uneasiness'. Having this mindset of 'struggle equals development and being uncomfortable is the price you pay for evolution' had a profound impact on people's ability to sit with the struggle and evolve their behaviour. And, as I talk about in great detail later in the book, the best news is that it's a teachable behaviour.

This finding came up in every cohort we studied who had implemented new and challenging behaviours. In a different study we worked with a client-facing division of a large financial institution where they were divided into four levels of performance. From best to worse, these levels were diamond, gold, silver and bronze. This performance measure was based on several factors, including achieving clear KPIs and also having a positive impact on their work culture and co-workers. In other words, their rating was a holistic one, rather than one just based on earnings.

When we asked them to rate how much challenge they had in their work, interestingly, the highest performing group perceived their work as being significantly more challenging than the poor performing group did (as shown in the following graph). So rather than getting to work thinking, *I have got this thing nailed*, the top performers were thinking, *My role has lots of challenge*.

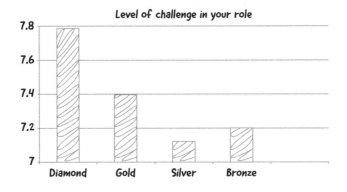

We found those in their company's diamond group were also particularly high in the strive response to struggle and challenge. They saw discomfort as the typical by-product of evolution. Rather than seeing these uncomfortable thoughts and emotions as a sign that they should retreat from them, they accepted those uncomfortable thoughts and feelings as part of the growth process.

Thanks to this mindset, even though the challenge was significantly higher for the diamond group, they scored higher on every single wellbeing measure we took. They were higher on fulfilment in life, and connection with people at work and outside of work, and were more satisfied with their quality of life. In addition, their level of positive emotion at work was through the roof, as you can see in the following graph.

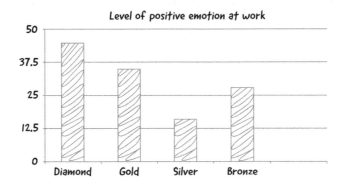

Finally, what was most interesting was their level of burnout was far lower, as shown in the next graph.

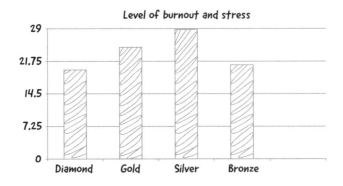

My research team and I found similar findings from a two-year training program and research project with the customer service division of a large organisation. Over this two-year period, we saw no change in the level of work challenge and work frustration for the employees, but we did see a significant improvement in enjoyment and satisfaction.

Put simply, their external world did not change significantly. The pressure and challenge associated with their work did not get any easier. (In fact, you could argue it had got more challenging because they went through a restructure in that time.) Work was still difficult and still led to frustration. However, after we taught them the strive strategies contained in this book, how emotionally drained they felt from work dropped by 26 per cent, their level of burnout dropped by 44 per cent and their enjoyment of work increased by 24 per cent. Again, the focus was not on removing challenge and pressure, but evolving people's response to it. And our findings again showed that having struggle and challenge in your life does not necessarily lead to poor wellbeing.

Our findings on this critical step of seeing struggle as an opportunity to develop rather than a threat have been backed up by other research. In a study by Graham Jones and Austin Swain (with the results published in 'Predispositions to experience debilitative and facilitative anxiety in elite and nonelite performers') showed that as they were about to compete, both elite and non-elite athletes experienced the presence of anxiety. However, the elite athletes perceived that the anxiety they felt improved their performance while the non-elite athletes saw the presence of anxiety as a bad thing and something that would make them perform worse.

Do it for your heart's sake

Our perception of struggle as either an opportunity to develop or a threat even affects our physical response to the situation. The amount of tension in our arteries and veins is defined as a measure called 'total peripheral resistance'. You could say it measures how stiff the walls of our cardiovascular system are. We don't want this measure to be high because when these walls are stiff, the heart has to work harder to push blood through and the increased pressure damages our arteries and veins. Studies have shown that, when we exercise, our heart does work harder and pumps more blood, but our very clever body relaxes our arteries and veins so 'total peripheral resistance' goes down in order to not do any damage.

In 'A theory of challenge and threat states in athletes' scientists Marc Jones, Carla Meijen, Paul Joseph McCarthy and David Sheffield showed that when we have a mindset that a challenge is an opportunity to develop and evolve, our cardiovascular system speeds up but we get a corresponding relaxation of our arteries and veins. This means the system becomes more active but relaxes at the same time so it doesn't get damaged. In contrast, when we see struggle and challenge as a threat, our body responds very differently. The cardiovascular system speeds up but total peripheral resistance is often shown to get worse. In other words, seeing struggle as a threat does damage to our cardiovascular system.

> **How we perceive struggle and challenge is critical to not only our performance but also our wellbeing.**

Under threat, our bodies also release cortisol, a steroid hormone. Most people think of cortisol as the 'stress hormone', but it has many functions beyond stress and is a very important chemical in your body. Your cortisol levels staying too high for too long, however, can lead to poor memory and concentration problems, heart disease, anxiety and depression, poor sleep and digestion as well as weight gain, particularly around your torso. Put bluntly, too much cortisol can make you fat and stupid.

Struggle and wellbeing can coexist

Michelle McQuaid completed a survey of 1002 Australian workers. She first asked, 'Considering everything that has happened over the last month, which of the following four categories would you put yourself in?'

- *Consistently thriving:* Feeling on top of the world; high in thriving and low in struggle.

- *Living well despite struggles:* High in thriving (meaning they had the knowledge, tools and support they need for wellbeing) but also high in struggle.

- *Not feeling bad but just getting by:* Low in thriving and low in struggle.

- *Really struggling:* Low in thriving (low in knowledge, tools and support they need for wellbeing) and high in struggle.

Michelle and her team then went on to measure various aspects of wellbeing and psychological constructs, to see how they correlated. What is interesting is that the 'living well despite struggles' group showed levels of wellbeing that were similar to the 'consistently thriving' group. Respondents reported significantly higher levels of wellbeing than those workers who were in the 'not feeling bad but just getting by' and 'really struggling' groups in the following measures:

- positive emotions
- engagement
- relationships
- meaning
- accomplishment
- job satisfaction
- health.

What this survey showed was that we don't have to remove challenge and struggle to improve people's wellbeing and quality of life. In fact, the presence of challenge and pressure is related to better wellbeing. The key factor is how people respond to that challenge and struggle.

Apply it to the ones we love the most

I am constantly amazed at how dumb I was a week ago. What I mean is I regularly have realisations where I give myself a face palm and think, *Why the hell have I been doing that?!* One such thought came to me recently.

I was on stage talking about my research and I was outlining a key finding around our relationship with struggle (describing what I've been discussing here—that the key to handling struggle is seeing the struggle as an opportunity to develop, not as a threat). Then it hit me like a bolt of lightning. For the previous couple of months we had been having issues with my daughter around her behaviour when she gets scared or anxious. From time to time, she would fall into destructive behaviours when she was highly stressed. Any sort of challenging behaviour with your children really drains you and hits you in your most vulnerable spot. We were struggling, and I found myself out of answers very quickly. But, as I was standing on stage in front of 1000 people, I realised that I was totally consumed in the threat response to this situation. I just wanted her to stop, I was demonising her, I didn't want to get in the trenches with this struggle, I just wanted it to go away and was looking at it as a huge inconvenience in my life. I was moving away from this situation, not moving towards it.

When I returned home, I totally reframed my approach to my daughter's behaviour. Talk about struggle; it was struggle on steroids. But I now approached it as, 'How do I have to evolve as a dad to handle this situation? What do I have to change, and who do I have to become?'—despite regularly wanting to retreat to blame and judgement. I stayed in the trenches with this struggle and worked on being compassionate and constructive and understanding. The impact was dramatic, and not only on me but also on my daughter. Sure we had setbacks and some days were a real shit fight, but my new approach had a profound impact on my behaviour and also hers. We were both calmer, and me focusing on my own evolution also reduced the passive-aggressive and tit-for-tat behaviours I had fallen into.

BRING STRUGGLE OUT OF THE SHADOWS

I chatted with Michelle McQuaid about her research and she shared a number of findings that supported my research. She also found people in her study saw struggle and stress as a bad thing or something they were aspiring to get rid of. However, Michelle also found that stress and struggle were critical to growth and development. She argued,

The more you give people permission to see that struggle is okay, the healthier and more constructive the response they have towards struggle. Many people have a huge sense of relief when they feel safe to admit that they are struggling and to realise they shouldn't feel guilty for experiencing it. People today feel pressure to have high wellbeing all the time. Wellbeing is not a constant upward trend; it fluctuates. We need more permission to discuss our struggles. Because of the positivity focus in society we don't talk about the negative things. If we don't address the negative side of things, how do we develop a healthier relationship with it?

Michelle has an amazing ability to articulate things clearly. She also highlighted,

When I am in the midst of struggle, it's my body's way of telling me that something here matters to me. In that moment, I try to bring curiosity to it to explore how I am feeling and what is going on for me.

I've already mentioned our school leader wellbeing project 'The Flourish Movement' and the four full-day workshops that are part of the program. At these workshops, we put the school leaders in small groups of 22 to 30 people, and encourage the participants to have real, vulnerable and authentic conversations.

Once you talk about and accept struggle, your relationship with it becomes far more constructive. The participants make comments such as, 'In my whole career, I have never had a conversation with a colleague about the fact that I am struggling with many parts of the job'. They talk about how empowering and freeing it is to do that. They mention that they feel collective permission that it is okay to not cope from time to time and that they shouldn't feel ashamed of experiencing that. One of the biggest breakthroughs comes from the fact that they realise everyone is struggling with something. Many people say things along the lines of, 'Wow, I thought I was the only one who was struggling. I thought everyone else had it together and it was just me who wasn't coping'.

> **Once you talk about and accept struggle, your relationship with it becomes far more constructive.**

SUMMARY

- The big difference between people who effectively strived and those who did not was their relationship with struggle. The people who strived saw struggle as an opportunity to develop and grow. People who did not strive saw struggle as a threat and retreated from it.

- Seeing struggle as an opportunity not only helps you overcome the struggle so you keep on striving but also reduces the negative stress response you can have to struggle.

- Having a functional relationship with struggle can lead to improvements in wellbeing, performance and enjoyment of work.

- Embracing struggle helps you to dramatically develop as a leader.

- The more you talk about your struggles and the more you bring them out in the open, the more positive your relationship with struggle and the more functional your response.

CHAPTER 8

Striving effectively: foreground behaviours

In our research exploring how people approach struggle, and how they can start to see it as an opportunity to develop rather than a threat, we examined many different groups of people. We looked at people in various organisations and various industries, and studied these groups to understand the common factors that helped them strive and handle struggle (known as a cross-sectional study). We then took these characteristics and trained different groups of people to get better at implementing them and measured if this increased their ability to strive and handle struggle over a long period (more than 12 months—known as a longitudinal study). Phew, enough science talk!

The good news is that it worked. The strategies I am about to share with you significantly increased people's capacity to manage struggle and strive more. And as I outlined in chapter 7 the first step in effective striving is the attitude that struggle equals development.

Seeing struggle as development

The good news is I'm not going to leave you with that little piece of advice. This chapter and the next focus on how you can see struggle as the pathway to development. Our research dug deeper to understand the psychological dynamics of this, and we found strivers have two layers of specific behaviours that allow them to sit in struggle and develop from it. I call these two layers foreground behaviours and background behaviours.

Foreground behaviours, which I cover in this chapter, are the behaviours you can do in the moment, in the trenches, to handle the struggle. Background behaviours, the focus of the next chapter, are the ritualised behaviours you can perform on a regular basis to set yourself up to handle struggle in a more constructive way and also create an environment that helps support you when dealing with struggle.

The function of the foreground behaviours is to be the stepping stone from struggle to development. When we are in the midst of struggle our emotions run high and our thoughts begin to catastrophise. These two things often derail our behaviour and lead us into dysfunction. We use the foreground behaviours to manage our thoughts and emotion so we can then execute constructive behaviours.

Too often we forget this step. When in struggle we are often told by others to focus on more positive thoughts and emotions or just do more helpful behaviours. Statements like 'don't think that', 'don't feel that way', 'why don't you just do this'. However this pragmatic and logical approach only works in very specific circumstances, because it assumes that humans constantly operate in a state of logic, which we do not (and anyone who has ever been in a romantic relationship with another person knows this). We are emotional creatures, not logical ones. I once saw a meme that said, 'Guys, when a woman is mad, just tell her she's overreacting. She'll realise you're right and calm right down'. Now, ignoring the condescending and misogynistic undertones of this, it illustrates that trying to be logical when we are under pressure is futile. The times when we need our response to be at its best are the times when we are most under pressure or challenged, and that is when emotion is at its highest.

This is the reason why we need the foreground behaviours. View them as the bridge between struggle and development.

I explore the three foreground behaviours in the following sections. The first is around acceptance—accepting that the struggle is going to feel uncomfortable and accepting your reaction to the struggle without judgement. The second is about connecting to the meaning and purpose that sits on the other side of the struggle—that is, connecting to the compelling reason as to why you want to tolerate and go through the discomfort. The third is about marvelling at your own courage.

Foreground behaviour #1: Accepting the struggle sucks, and being okay with your reaction

To put it crudely, true strivers willingly climbed into the trenches with struggle and accepted that it was going to suck. They were under no delusions about the discomfort they were going to take on. They didn't see the discomfort as a sign that they shouldn't take on that struggle.

For too long we have been sold on the message that to overcome a challenging situation or to exhibit a challenging behaviour, we need to bring a positive mindset and emotion to it. For example, say you want to do a new and difficult behaviour, but when you think of it you experience negative thoughts and emotions. We have been taught that in order to do that behaviour, the critical next step is to shift your mindset and emotions to make them positive. The following figure sums this up.

> **True strivers willingly climbed into the trenches with struggle and accepted that it was going to suck.**

This linear model is being challenged by various research, including mine. In our research, my team and I found that strivers weren't limited to the presence of a positive mindset and positive emotions. Instead, strivers were able to tolerate the discomfort of the difficult thoughts and feelings and still take effective action.

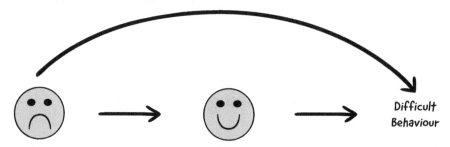

We also found that strivers don't judge their reaction to the struggle, but instead accept whatever reaction comes up for them when they are experiencing discomfort. By 'reaction' I mean the thoughts and emotions that come up amid the struggle.

Psychology and self-help guides have traditionally argued that certain thoughts and emotions are good and certain thoughts and emotions are bad—and that you should keep the good ones and get rid of the bad ones. Rather than getting caught up in their reaction and determining if it was useful or not, however, strivers accepted their reaction without judgement and focused on the most constructive action they could take in that moment.

This links in with the research being done in the area of acceptance and commitment therapy (ACT), also often referred to as psychological flexibility. This therapy is based on the theory that the thoughts and emotions you think and feel about a situation are largely irrelevant. They are simply thoughts and emotions. Instead of trying to change your reaction, you should instead accept whatever thoughts and emotions come up for you and focus on taking action that aligns to your values. The research in this area has been building strongly and the use of ACT has been shown to not only help people manage debilitating pathology such as anxiety, OCD and depression, but also increase our capacity to deal with struggle and difficult thoughts and feelings. A key component of ACT is complete acceptance of our thoughts and feelings. When you accept your reaction to a stressful event without judgement, you reduce the impact that the stressful event has on you.

Say you are about to sit an exam and due to its importance you are extremely nervous. As you sit down to take the test, waves of anxiety wash over you. Your thoughts start to race: *What if I screw up this exam? I haven't studied enough. I am not prepared for this. I suck at exams.* Due to your thoughts, your anxiety shifts into full-blown panic. Your thoughts start to compound and build on themselves.

Let's look at what happens next depending on whether you accept or judge your thoughts and emotions.

Judging your thoughts

On top of the panic and racing thoughts, you now add judgement in there. *Why do I get so nervous? I am so weak! Why can't I stay calm? To do well in an exam, you have to be calm. I should be confident. I am a loser. OMG, if I don't calm down I am going to have a full-blown panic attack and totally screw this up. Calm down, stop freaking out. Be more positive.*

In this situation, you have to deal with not only doing well in the exam and your panic about the situation, but now also the judgement of your reaction—which only pours petrol on this volatile situation. Judging your reaction to a situation as wrong or bad just adds another thing you have to deal with and increases your chance of doing an ineffective behaviour.

Accepting your thoughts instead

As you sit down to take the test, waves of anxiety wash over you. Your thoughts start to race, but instead of judging those thoughts your reaction is, *Of course I am feeling anxious. I am about to do an exam and I find this situation really stressful. When I get stressed, I tend to blow things out of proportion and my thoughts race.*

You accept the fact that you are going to predict disaster and catastrophise the situation and, because you are not trying to stop your reaction, you have space to focus on doing constructive behaviours. While you can't stop these thoughts, what you can do is accept that they are there and then focus your mind on a behaviour that would improve your performance. For example, you could slow your breathing down or breathe in for four counts and out for six counts. Another helpful behaviour could be calming your mind by focusing your attention on one sensation, such as how your feet feel against your shoes or how the texture of the desk feels against your hands. When you are not trying to fight your thoughts, you have space to focus your attention on far more constructive behaviours that help calm you and align your thought processes. Also, your acceptance of your thoughts and feelings reduces their power and control over you. I really need to emphasise this point. As it was such a strong finding in our research. When you accept your response to struggle without judgement, the stress itself has less impact on you and you are able to more rapidly move onto better behaviours.

This same approach of accepting rather than judging can be used in any situation where you find yourself struggling with negative thought and emotion—from feeling self-conscious at a party to lacking confidence before a job interview or asking for a promotion.

> **When you are not trying to fight your thoughts, you have space to focus your attention on far more constructive behaviours.**

Following a presentation a woman came up to me and said, 'My 13-year-old daughter is a national level long jumper. How do I stop her getting nervous before a jump?' I asked her why she wanted to stop her getting nervous, and she replied, 'Because when she gets nervous, she starts to panic, she can't think straight and she jumps terribly. I need to stop her getting nervous.'

I said, 'Every athlete I know in the world gets nervous before they compete. What is more constructive is if she views her nerves as a normal part of competition. Rather than trying to make them go away, she can accept them and focus on the process she goes through before a jump. This will help her respond far more effectively to her nerves'.

We often make the mistake of thinking anxiety before any type of performance is detrimental. However, researchers Graham Jones and Austin Swain have shown that anxiety only detracts from performance when the person has the mindset that anxiety is a bad thing. In their studies, athletes who accepted their anxiety as a natural part of competing were not held back by their anxiety. In contrast, athletes who thought being anxious before competition was a bad thing saw a significant drop in performance when they got anxious.

THE EVOLUTION OF PERFORMANCE PSYCHOLOGY

Richard Fryer is a performance psychologist who has worked with Olympic-level athletes. I interviewed him on how performance psychology has evolved, and here is what he had to say.

How we manage performance under pressure has evolved dramatically. The old way (that most of us are familiar with) was around self-talk control (making sure you were saying positive things to yourself) and imagining perfect performance. This approach focused on eradicating any negative thought and emotion that was believed to limit performance. Put simply, 'Fix your head and you fix your performance'. The problem with this approach is when things are going great, things go great. In other words, when you are confident, your performance is good. However, when you are not in a good space, your performance drops. The approach of trying to control our thoughts and emotions leads to inconsistent performance.

The new approach is focused on seeing a separation between our thoughts and feelings and our performance. This means people can perform well under any circumstances, rather than waiting to be in a good head space before being able to perform. We focus on getting athletes to realise that their thoughts and feelings before an event are not a good indicator of how they will perform.

> **How Richard uses acceptance with athletes is getting them not to judge or demonise certain thoughts and feelings. He says,**
>
> When athletes accept whatever thoughts and feelings come up for them, the experiences they are trying to avoid decrease. They don't experience as much anxiety, and they don't experience as much tension. In contrast, when they are trying to control or get rid of those thoughts and feelings, their anxiety and tension go up. What really brings athletes undone are two things. The first is having the mindset that they should feel a certain way. The fact that an athlete feels demotivated or anxious is not the problem. The problem is when they believe they should feel more motivated or more confident to be able to perform. The second issue is comparing themselves to their competition and believing they are experiencing much healthier thoughts and emotions. They think, for example, *I bet my competition aren't feeling doubt or fear. It's just me. They are in a much better state than me.* Normative comparison really brings people undone. When they believe that everyone else is cool, calm and collected, they want to control their own thoughts and feelings more.
>
> All athletes feel doubt and fear. When they accept their responses without judgement and stop trying to change their thoughts and feelings, their performance increases and is more consistent.

Foreground behaviour #2: Connecting to meaning and purpose

Over the past five years, I've had a love/hate relationship with meaning and purpose. The reason is that meaning and purpose are everywhere and everyone is talking about them. Thanks to Simon Sinek (who I think is brilliant), everyone believes that having a clear 'why' is the answer to all their problems and the thing that will ensure their unlimited success. As with all things that become popular, however, this has been bastardised and become trite. Every organisation is now talking about their 'why'—they put it on their websites and plaster it all over their walls. In every ad on TV, organisations are shoving it down our throats.

The reason you're perhaps sensing a sarcastic and cynical tone is that most of these organisations act in a way that is completely misaligned to their 'why'. I'm not saying having those statements is bad, but don't put them up on your wall or profess them unless you're going to live aligned to them. Countless financial institutions, for example, claim to be customer-centric and that their 'why' is to protect and enable the financial wellbeing of every customer, yet when it comes down to choosing between profits and their 'why', many seem to screw the customer every single time. Yeah, I'm pretty jaded when it comes to meaning and purpose. So jaded, in fact, that I secretly hoped that our research would tell us that meaning and purpose wasn't that important, and, as a result, we could launch an anti–meaning and purpose campaign. (Okay, I'm really jaded when it comes to meaning and purpose.)

Unfortunately (for me), our data on striving showed having a strong meaning and purpose on the other side of struggle is the greatest tool to helping you handle the discomfort that comes with courage and evolution. Damn it! Don't you hate it when you are wrong?! But that's the problem with science—you have to go where the data takes you.

But I didn't go down without a fight, because my team and I discovered a few things in our research around how we have gotten meaning and purpose wrong. First of all, far too much judgement and too many rules are in place around meaning and purpose. We often think that meaning and purpose only exist in this huge altruistic frame where to have true meaning and purpose we need to be rescuing orphaned kittens or curing cancer.

Also, we've been led to believe that we only have one 'why', and that people have to discover their big 'why'. Multiple websites and programs available for purchase offer to help you find your 'why'. This is all too limiting, however, because we don't just find meaning and purpose in one area of our lives. In fact, buying into this ideology can actually make you monomaniacal, as you become obsessed and fanatical about one concept. Meaning and purpose is far too big and complex a concept to be simplified down to a snappy one-line statement. My research team and I found that meaning and purpose existed in multiple contexts and on multiple levels. The different levels were:

- achievement of a goal
- mastery of a skill
- contribution to others.

Achievement of a goal and mastery connect to the evolution part of striving that I discussed in chapter 4, so let's start there!

Goal achievement

Our data showed that goal achievement can give people tremendous meaning and purpose. Now if you have been paying attention, you are probably thinking, *Hold on, this sounds a bit shallow and, well, isn't this the completion myth?* And you would be right. While achievement of a goal is not as fulfilling as a deep altruistic meaning and purpose or the evolution we witness in the strive, goal achievement can still motivate us to push through struggle. Extrinsic goals are not useless; you just don't want to put all your eggs in that one basket. For example, you may have a goal to run a half marathon (I write this as a person who would rather watch question time in politics than go for a run) and the meaning you have attached to the achievement of that goal can help you overcome the struggle associated with getting up early in the cold, pulling on your runners and hitting the pavement. Likewise, the desire to clear your to-do list by the end of the day can help you push through the struggle when your motivation starts to wane. Don't dismiss the power of achievement.

ACHIEVEMENT AND MOTIVATION

A number of years ago, I had a healthcare arm to my business, which focused on helping people with chronic disease (such as diabetes, heart disease and cholesterol problems) implement lifestyle change that would help their condition. I had one of my best corporate clients call me and ask if I would help with his mother-in-law who had bad diabetes. I explained to him that I no longer worked in that part of the business and that she would be better off seeing one of our staff. He said, 'Look, she is a difficult case and doesn't like seeing doctors. However, she has seen some of your YouTube videos and has agreed to go see you. It would be a huge favour to me'.

Because he was such a great guy, I agreed to meet Sue, his mother-in-law. I looked at her blood work and her latest test results and saw she was in a terrible way. The diabetes was starting to have an impact on her vision, the nerves in her feet and also her heart. I said to her, 'This is obviously not a surprise to you, but unless you start making some lifestyle changes, you are going to get very sick, very quickly'.

She said, 'Yeah, I get all of that but I literally just don't want to do it. I don't enjoy the exercise and I don't enjoy the food that will help me manage my diabetes better. My family are on my back about this constantly but I have tried everything and it's really of no interest'. I was straight with her and told her I wasn't going to take her money because I knew she wouldn't stick to what I would ask her to do, and so we shouldn't waste our time on this anymore.

About six months later, I got a call from Sue and she said things had changed, and she now wanted to do what was required. She came to my office and sat down across the table from me and I asked what was so different. She said, 'I have a four-year-old granddaughter who was over playing the other day, running around the backyard. Now, I am not mobile enough to run around with her so I sat in a chair and watched her run around. She was pretending to be a plane or a princess or something when all of a sudden she stopped in front of me, looked me in the eyes and said, "You're not as much fun as my other grandmother because you don't run around and play with me'". Sue then very calmly said, 'At that moment something in my head snapped and I thought, *That bitch is not going to be the favourite!*' Since our meeting, Sue has gone from strength to strength — and all that changed was that she now had a compelling reason for putting up with the discomfort of changing her lifestyle. She wanted to achieve something that meant a hell of a lot to her.

Obtaining mastery

The next aspect connected to meaning and purpose is mastery of a skill. This fits far more into the intrinsic goal category, where you are focusing on being more masterful at something. The meaning and purpose attached to mastery is simply seeing yourself evolve and grow, and the reward is the mastery. You are not mastering the skill to go up in anyone's esteem or to win a prize or praise. You are pursuing mastery because you enjoy the process itself. Individuals we studied said that they found tremendous levels of meaning and purpose in the pursuit of mastery and that witnessing themselves become more masterful was enormously meaningful for them.

Let me explain mastery another way. To achieve any goal you can be motivated by three main drivers:

1. *To win:* This is where we want the prize on the other side of the goal. Whether that prize is money, setting a record, the admiration of others or knowing that we are better than our competitors, we are driven by what winning will give us.

2. *To not lose:* This is where we don't care about winning, we just don't want to come last. The big driver here is we want to be safe, and we don't want to look stupid.

3. *To obtain mastery:* This is where our driver is to get better at the task, and our reward is the development of skill. Winning

would be nice but the real motivation is how we become more skilful.

Research shows that people who focus on mastery are not only far more resilient to struggle and setback, but also progress their skill level faster and achieve better performance. In addition, they find the activity far more rewarding and engaging.

> People who focus on mastery are not only far more resilient to struggle and setback, but also progress their skill level faster and achieve better performance.

MASTERING THE ART OF BASKETBALL

A great example of being driven by mastery is by John Wooden, who is considered one of the greatest sports coaches to ever live. He coached college basketball for UCLA, winning ten national championships in a 12-year period — seven of them in a row (the next closest team won four in a row). His win percentage was over 80 per cent.

When asked why his team was so successful, he said, 'Because we never talked about winning or losing; we only focused on mastering the art of basketball'. Before every match, each player would pick their mastery focus for that match. This was the thing they would do 1 per cent better than when they last played. At the end of every match, they would sit round in a circle and debrief how they felt they had done in their attempt to master that part of the game.

Wooden was quoted as saying, 'You should not know whether my team had won or lost by how they walk out of the change rooms. This is not about winning or losing; this is about mastering our craft'. He had his team focus on continual improvement rather than the score board and the rest took care of itself.

Deliberate practice drives mastery

Another validation of the importance of mastery comes from the 10 000-hour rule. You've likely heard of this principle, popularised by journalist Malcolm Gladwell in his book *Outliers*. In the book, Gladwell details that to be world-class at something you must put in 10000 hours of practice. This concept came from a 1993 paper written by Anders Ericsson, a professor at the University of Colorado, called 'The role of deliberate practice in the acquisition of expert performance'.

Unfortunately, Gladwell didn't report the whole picture from the research, because it was not just the volume of practice that differentiated the high performers (and, in fact, most researchers agree that the figure of 10000 hours is not accurate, it is thought to be far higher) but also how they practised. The world-class performers always practised in an uncomfortable state, and in a way that made them focus on the subtle improvements they would achieve in that session. In other words, they continually focused on mastery. In every practice session, they would set out to focus on the mastery of a specific aspect of a skill.

One of the most beautiful examples of mastery I've seen is while watching a friend of mine, Colin James, present. Colin is a sight to see, and every time I watch him, I want to run home and start practising. He is elegant, considered and so beautiful to watch. How he has achieved this is that he is constantly studying presenters of all forms (comedians, magicians, singers, poets—you name it, Colin has analysed it). I was talking to him about this and he said in the early days he would spend thousands of hours practising at home, but that most of his practice now is done on stage. He said, 'Every time before I walk out in front of an audience, I choose one thing that I will spend that presentation mastering. It could be pausing, or using different parts of the stage, or my hand gestures or vocal intonation. Every time I walk off stage, I am a better presenter than when I walked on'.

If volume of practice was all that was required, my mum would be a world-class racing car driver by now, because she has easily driven for 10000 hours. Why is she not a highly skilled driver? Because when she drives she is not thinking about skill acquisition or how to improve this tiny little bit of her driving, she is simply going through the motions.

When we develop a skill we move through four specific stages:

1. *Unconscious incompetence*: This is where you don't know you don't have the skill, and you are not aware of your incompetence. Using learning to drive as an example, you have never driven before and you don't know how difficult it is and you don't know if you can do it.

2. *Conscious incompetence:* This is where you realise you are not very good at that skill. You try to drive and you are terrible at it and you realise you need lots and lots of practice to become competent.

3. *Conscious competence:* This is where you can perform the skill but it takes a lot of concentration and effort. You can drive but you're always concentrating and you never take your eyes off the road.

4. *Unconscious competence:* This is where you can do the skill easily, it has become a habit, and it no longer requires concentration and effort. You can drive home and have no recollection of how you got there. You don't consciously think about driving, you just do it.

The problem with unconscious competence is that it stops you progressing with the skill; you just go into autopilot and cruise. Now that might be fine for some tasks but that doesn't help you become more masterful at what you are doing. In addition, unconscious competence does not help you deal with struggle. In fact, it tends to make struggle worse because your mind is no longer on the task and so it naturally drifts to worry and rumination. When you are no longer present and conscious of your progress and mastery, you make struggle worse.

Staying in conscious competence

To be truly present with your own progress and mastery, stay in conscious competence. It is where you are paying attention to actively improving your skills.

Let me explain this through a case study. I was working with an organisation that had a large in-store presence and which was trying to reengineer the experience customers had when they came into the store—because the current experience people had in the store was not a good one. The salespeople were incentivised to hit large sales targets by pushing products onto customers, whether they needed the product or not.

Instead, the organisation wanted the salesperson to collaborate with the customer to co-create a solution that would give them the best possible outcome. This new process required salespeople to have a different conversation with customers. Rather than telling them what they needed, they now asked them what they were looking for, how much they wanted to spend and what the final outcome they desired was. Then the salesperson would put together a plan and implement that plan for the customer. Sounds pretty straightforward, doesn't it?

While the business thought it would be easy for the salespeople to implement this new experience, they discovered it was incredibly difficult. The salespeople were freaking out, were failing at the task and leaving customers with a weird experience, and no-one was happy. You could say that this company was experiencing struggle on steroids, and the salespeople were looking at that struggle as a threat. Their focus was on, 'What if I screw this up?', 'What if I can't handle it?', 'What if I can't evolve and change?', 'What if they fire me?'

In order to support the salespeople and help them overcome this struggle and achieve the desired outcome, the company turned to the strategy of using meaning, purpose, and mastery.

Firstly, they increased their internal communications around why the organisation was making this change, and how it would benefit salespeople and the customer. And they had their managers reassure the salespeople that the change would take time and the managers were there to help.

Secondly, the organisation mapped out a new experience of dealing with the customer, step-by-step from start to finish.

The process had four parts:

1. *Engage:* Understand the customer's needs and wants.

2. *Customise:* Come up with a personalised plan for the customer.

3. *Implement:* Ensure that everything was in place with the order and all the admin was correct.

4. *Check in:* Check in with the customer and keep the relationship alive.

Each of these parts had many steps. For example, 'Engage' consisted of:

- greet
- build rapport
- clarify
- question
- educate
- guide.

Each salesperson then took the entire plan, determined which areas they wanted to work on first, and filled out a mastery map on the specific things they were working on. As soon as they felt they had the right level of mastery in that area, they moved on to another part of the process. To add further support the managers installed whiteboards in the back office and, each week, the salespeople would put up their mastery focus. This enabled the managers to check in and coach the salespeople on their chosen mastery focus, and discuss with them how they had progressed and evolved.

And the results were staggering. The skill acquisition of the salespeople was incredibly fast and keeping track of their progress heavily engaged them in the process so they stayed motivated. Profits rose dramatically as did customer satisfaction

An unexpected benefit was that, after the implementation of this program, they also saw the gap between the best salespeople and the worst salespeople reduce. The poor performers dramatically increased their performance and, at the same time, their engagement and satisfaction at work dramatically rose. This is a great example of how motivating mastery can be.

Contribution to others

The final area—contribution to others—is the most compelling when it comes to meaning and purpose. This is a classic area we think of whenever the subject of meaning and purpose is brought up—that is, how do our actions contribute to and improve the lives of other people? As I discussed earlier in this chapter, however, we've been too rigid and short-sighted when it comes to meaning and purpose. We should not just have one area of contribution. This is not *Lord of the Rings* with one ring to rule them all. Likewise, there is not one 'why' to rule them all. Multiple levels of contribution help us push through struggle and continue to strive. For example, your big overarching 'why' around contribution could be one of the following:

- helping women achieve pay equity
- helping organisations follow more sustainable business practices to reduce their impact on the environment
- encouraging teachers to evolve their practices so they consider the learning preferences and capabilities of each child in their class.

These sorts of big 'why' statements are great to give us direction and to motivate us. However, my team's research showed that contributing to others in a small way was just as helpful in overcoming struggle and challenge. For example, say your big 'why' is 'to improve the financial literacy and habits of women in Australia so they can be more independent and control their destiny'. However, in your small business you have to have a hard conversation with a staff member because of their negative impact on the culture of the business. This conversation is going to require courage from you, because hard conversations bring with them a shit tonne of struggle.

In that moment, you could draw a pretty long bow as to how this conversation is helping you get closer to your big overarching 'why'. However, a more constructive way to handle the struggle is to tap into a more immediate and proximal contribution. For example, you could focus on how dealing with that struggle will make a significant contribution to the rest of your staff. You dealing with that struggle and holding that person to account for their behaviour will contribute to the other team members having a better experience at work and greater trust in you, and so improve their quality of life, job satisfaction, feeling of safety at work and engagement.

> Every time you go through struggle while you are striving, ask yourself: what is the meaning and purpose on the other side of this discomfort?

Don't just be limited to one version of meaning and purpose. Every time you go through struggle while you are striving, ask yourself: what is the meaning and purpose on the other side of this discomfort? You have the following to choose from and focus on:

- How will this action take you closer to your big, headline meaning and purpose?

- How will this action make a contribution to other people and benefit others? In a big or a small way?

- How will this action make you more masterful and skilful?

- How will this action take you closer to the goal you want to achieve?

CONTRIBUTION AND SCHOOL LEADERS

The greatest example I have of contribution allowing people to push through struggle is The Flourish Movement. School leaders are truly amazing. Theirs is one of the hardest jobs I have ever studied in over 20 years of research. They have so many stakeholders they have to keep happy, huge workloads and a job that is so incredibly broad they have to wear many hats. One minute they could be dealing with a maintenance issue, and the next they have a meeting with an irate parent, then they have to observe a teacher and give them performance feedback, meet with their director about their school strategic plan, and then have a hard conversation with a staff member about their conduct.

Highlighting this even more, a principal once sent me this breakdown of their day:

- 8.30 am: Difficult conversation with an executive; very stressful and they were very upset but in the end resolved.

- 8.50 am: Meeting with new student and parent; student on partial exemption due to anxiety disorder which manifests as aggressive and non-compliant behaviours.

- 9.00 am: Meeting with a dad whose wife passed away on Saturday.

- 9.25 am: Dad had left; I cried then went to check on the two little boys whose mummy died. They are such gorgeous boys. Christ this breaks my heart.

- 10.00 am: Rang FACS (family and community services) as two children at risk have not turned up at school.

- 10.20 am: Receive email from parent with many not strongly veiled threats about who she's going to advise about a casual teacher who has allegedly manhandled her son.

And then the rest of the day, the hits just continued.

As this shows the job can get pretty dark. One the most upsetting and disturbing stories I have ever heard was about a principal who had to comfort a mother whose husband had murdered their two children and then killed himself. She sat with this woman for hours comforting her, and they were both sobbing. Can you even imagine? After the police came to collect her, the principal said she looked at her watch and realised it was five minutes before she was due to go to an assembly and hand out awards to children. She said, 'I stood up, shook myself off, and went out and was all smiles for the kids and the parents'.

Add to this the facts that principals rarely get thanked at the end of the year and that the rates of physical and verbal abuse of principals have greatly increased. You wonder what keeps them putting up with all that struggle, don't you?

What keeps them going is the kids, and their sense of contribution to the children. I've worked with hundreds of school leaders over the past three years, and what they have in common is they would all lie down in traffic for their school. They see their role as a true calling and their connection to the contribution they make enables them to sit with any struggle the job throws up for them. But at the same time we found that mastery and achievement of specific goals were often still powerful motivators that helped them put up with the many struggles that come with the job.

CONNECTING TO MEANING AND PURPOSE

I did some work for a large medical device company that I thought had amazing alignment to their meaning and purpose. The reality is that their devices save countless lives every year. What this company does really well is show every single person in the company how their actions enable this meaning and purpose. And this strong connection to the patient really helped the organisation through a very challenging time. A few years ago, they acquired another large medical supply company, which effectively doubled the size of their business. If you've experienced trying to merge two large companies, you know what a colossal task this is. Even if you haven't, you can probably imagine the significant struggles that came up.

I interviewed their delightful and brilliant HR Director about this time. She said,

> We had two big challenges. The obvious one was how do you get two cultures to come together and break down the 'us and them' mentality? The second one was the operational challenges in the merge — we had IT issues, systems issues and supply chain issues. This, obviously, affected our ability to get our product out to medical professionals and hospitals. Put these two challenges together and they are simply massive. We started to see people fall into dysfunctional behaviours and the narrative in many teams was, 'This is too hard'. In response to this we did two things. First of all, we really drove home the message of why people are working there, and the meaning and purpose that sits behind the company.

To address this huge issue they reminded people about the company's purpose. They introduced culture circles where the teams talked about the meaning and purpose in their job (the most discussed topic was improving patient outcomes). They showcased patients in multiple forums. They had some come into the office and talk to the staff about the impact of their products on their lives. They had patients speak at their conferences. They sent out videos about patient stories. She told me one story of a young father who needed a heart transplant. While waiting for a donor he used one of their products (an external heart) to keep him alive. Following his successful transplant operation, they did a follow-up story on him so all the staff knew what happened. They also increased how much time the teams interacted face to face, not just over email, and they increased time that people could take off work to volunteer for charities that were aligned to the work the company does.

She said, 'This strong connection to meaning and purpose helped the two organisations come together to find a common ground'.

What was fascinating is that she said you can only rely on meaning and purpose for so long: 'You also have to be seen to be doing something'. Which is what they did. They threw huge resources at solving the systems and supply chain issues, and also introduced more bottom-up decision-making, asking people on the frontlines using the systems to help design the new systems. Allowing people to give input and have a sense of control over the future was a critically important step.

What was the impact of these two actions? Staff turnover in the company was less than the industry average, and in some areas of the business was less than 4 per cent. Also, when they had system issues, people volunteered to work weekends and nights to do logistics. Vice presidents and senior leaders even flew in from all over the country to help pack and label boxes and then send them out. It was all hands on deck.

She said,

> It was our strong connection to meaning and purpose that allowed us to handle the significant struggle that we were going through. Now that we are through it, we look back on that time with such a huge sense of pride at what we achieved.

Finally, on a personal note, she said that when things got really hard, as we all naturally do, she started to think, *Do I have the ability to handle this? Should I just leave and look for something easier?* Her strong attachment to the meaning and purpose enabled her to stay in the trenches with the struggle.

The final word from her is this:

> If you are going to focus on meaning and purpose as a company, it has to be genuine because people have a finely tuned BS detector on this sort of thing.

Foreground behaviour #3: Marvelling at your own courage

The third behaviour that helped people use struggle as a stepping stone to development was when people focused on the courage they would have to display or were already displaying. Our key finding here was that in the throes of struggle, both strategies were effective. Let's look at both approaches a little more.

Focusing on the courage that would be required to handle the struggle works because, when we frame the required behaviour as courage, we are immediately more engaged and in a more action-based mindset. In contrast, if we frame it around the fear we must overcome, we are far less likely to tolerate the struggle.

The second strategy involved people reflecting on the courage that they were already displaying in the trenches with struggle. Witnessing our own courage is a deeply moving experience and in turn inspires us to display more courage.

As I have detailed earlier in this book, we crave to be courageous and a lack of courage is often one of our greatest regrets. In terms of using courage to sit with discomfort, my team's research showed that when people are in the trenches with struggle the very simple act of paying attention to and reflecting on courage gives them a shield that stops struggle from knocking them down. Even small moments of courage can serve this purpose—you don't have to be running into a burning building or putting your life on the line to exhibit courage.

Some examples people gave in our research were:

- having the courage to give my boss feedback on how they talk to me

- having the courage to ask my partner for intimacy

- having the courage to raise my hand in a meeting and put forward my idea

- having the courage to not drink wine and eat chocolate after a hard day at work

- having the courage to not blow up at my kids when they are driving me crazy.

In some of our programs, we gave people a 30-day courage challenge. As you can likely gather from the name, every day for 30 days they had to do one activity that required courage. We also asked them to document how they felt and what happened.

Other websites and authors talk about similar concepts—for example, rejection challenges where every day you had to be rejected by another human being. Entrepreneur Tim Ferris, famous as an author and a podcaster, advocates practising being uncomfortable, and suggests activities like going into a coffee shop, lying down on the floor and letting people walk around or over you, fasting for three days to experience real hunger, or asking for a discount whenever you buy food, clothes or even coffee. Other ideas are attempting to live on $15 per week or camping out on your friend's floor for a week in just a sleeping bag.

However, our research showed that to be more courageous you don't have to do ridiculous or extremely uncomfortable behaviours such as these. The problem with these types of approaches is they tend to put off the average person and they dismiss them as gimmicky and stupid. My other problem is these activities rarely improve your quality of life. You are effectively being uncomfortable for the sake of being uncomfortable. You're far better off attaching some sort of purpose to each of your desired courageous behaviours.

Some things I suggested to people were:

- At work, sit in a different part of the business from what you normally do so you get to know and understand different people and functions. This will require courage and also have real, tangible benefits.

- Share your ideas in a meeting when you normally keep them to yourself.

- Give someone at work you don't know a compliment—for example, 'Awesome presentation last week, I learned a lot. Super helpful'.

- Say hi to people in the elevator.

- While you are having lunch in the staff room, start up conversations with people you don't normally talk to.

- Try an activity that goes against your self-image—if you think you're un-coordinated, try dance classes; if you think you're not funny, enrol in a comedy course; if you think you're not artistic, try a drawing class.

- Volunteer for a charity.

- Interact with a group you don't mix with but have judged from afar—for example, go to a shelter and help the homeless to give you a different perspective.

- Call a friend you haven't seen for a long time or, even better, make up with a friend you had a falling out with.

Practise being courageous but choose activities that will have a beneficial impact on your life, not just those that make you uncomfortable for the sake of it.

Applying the strive process to real situations

Over the next few tables, I outline some case studies that emerged from our data. The data came from forms we had our research participants fill out, which broke down the areas of strive and struggle as shown in the tables.

Small business strive

The current situation	I am a leader of a small business and I've realised I spend far too much time putting out fires, solving problems and rescuing my staff when they have an issue. My team seem to feel they need to run every decision and issue past me directly. And I spend far too much time on email and in meetings.

The strive	I want to evolve into a leader who: • consistently works on the areas of more importance, actually getting to the big strategic issues • coaches my people to solve their own issues and challenges • empowers my team to take responsibility for their decisions • gives the team great clarity around the vision for the business and the results I want them to achieve • leaves them alone once they have this clarity so they can do it their way.
The struggle	• Letting go of control and trusting that the team will get the right outcome. • Resisting the urge to nitpick and pull apart their work when this doesn't add value or make the outcome better. • Accepting that they will do it differently from me, which doesn't mean it is wrong. • Not freaking out and getting angry when they make a mistake or drop the ball on something.
How to embrace the struggle and see it as development	
Acceptance	I realise that this experience will bring up all sorts of negative thoughts and emotions for me. I will predict disaster and say things like, 'I am losing control of the business'. I will feel lazy for stepping back from the frantic activity. I will come up with all sorts of reasons for needing to go back to my old ways. I need to accept that this is one of the biggest challenges leaders all over the world face in their business. I will relapse. I will not see these thoughts and feelings as a reason to give up on my strive. The suck will be massive, and it will probably never go away. I will sit with the discomfort.

Meaning and purpose (made up of contribution, mastery or achievement of a goal)	
Contribution	I want to progress the business and structure it in a way so that I can move down to four days a week. This is very important for my family but with the current way of working it is impossible. I want to feel like a more involved and connected parent. Overcoming this struggle and striving for my desired outcome will transform the culture and capability of my team. People enjoy work far more when they are trusted, have autonomy and get more stimulating responsibility.
Mastery	I will develop mastery through: • increasing my ability to communicate a clear vision around my desired outcome, and to provide clear guidelines they need to work within to achieve that • improving my capacity to develop systems that the team can follow • developing my coaching skills, which can then be used in multiple contexts.
Courage	Changing my interactions, having different conversations, having higher expectations of people, standing up in front of people saying, 'This is our vision and here is how I need your help' is incredibly courageous. It will add so much to my self-worth. Also saying no to opportunities that sit outside my vision so I stay on my chosen path takes great courage.

Dysfunctional culture strive

The current situation	I am a leader of a team whose culture is not a functional or constructive one, and it's having a negative impact on the performance and fulfilment of the team.
The strive	I want to create clarity around the sort of culture I want to see in the team, and communicate that clarity to them. I want to have a culture in my team where people have open, transparent and authentic conversations, rather than having conversations behind other people's backs. In addition, I would like the team to get to the point where they keep each other accountable for upholding the culture.
The struggle	• Having a good hard look at myself and reflecting on how I have contributed to creating the dysfunctional culture. Taking a stand on culture is a very vulnerable act because it exposes some of the shortcomings in my behaviour. • Having difficult conversations with people and holding them accountable for their behaviour. • Once I have articulated the cultural vision for the team, drawing a line in the sand, holding firm on that and ensuring my behaviour is aligned to that new vision. If I screw up and don't act that way, having to apologise and do better next time.
How to embrace the struggle and see it as development	
Acceptance	Oh boy, this will be huge. I struggle with hard conversations and before them I predict disaster and get quite anxious. I try to talk myself out of them. Also, I find it hard to admit when I make mistakes to my team. I worry that they will think I don't know what I am doing. Rather than getting caught up in my thoughts and emotions, I promise to accept that they will be there but they will not stop me taking action.

Meaning and purpose (made up of contribution, mastery or achievement of a goal)	
Contribution	Everyone wants a team with a lower level of politics and back stabbing. Any progress in this area will dramatically increase the connection and safety of my team. A feeling of safety increases people's performance, their satisfaction and general wellbeing. Going through this process will enable me to learn so much about myself and my leadership. This self-awareness will enable me to help future teams I lead and increase my likelihood of more senior roles. My team could become a shining light in our organisation around what is possible for team culture, and my team could be the new benchmark. As a result, I could have the best talent wanting to join my team.
Mastery	I will develop mastery through: • having a hard conversation with team members if they act in a way that is misaligned to the new desired culture • genuinely listening to their responses and considering them • communicating clearly and compassionately my concerns and what I expect from people in the team around their behaviour.
Courage	Nothing is more courageous than owning your shit and taking responsibility for what you have created. I will also show the courage to believe that it is possible for my team to get there. Having hard conversations with people around their behaviour, rather than avoiding those conversations or rationalising poor behaviour, takes serious guts.

Working mum strive

The current situation	I am a busy working mum with a stressful job, a husband who travels and three kids. Apart from the usual demands of life each of the kids has a lot of activities. When I am not working, I am running them all over the place. The logistics involved to manage the kids feel very similar to organising the G20! As a result, I feel like a terrible mother and I never get a moment to myself.
The strive	I want time back to do something for myself. Also I want to be more present with the kids and feel like I am engaging with them rather than rushing them from one activity to another.
The struggle	• I feel incredibly guilty when I take time for myself. • I find it hard to say 'no' to others. • I feel that I need to take care of everyone else. • I have to recognise that I am not superwoman and that at some stage I am going to burn out.
How to embrace the struggle and see it as development	
Acceptance	I have to accept that the guilt of doing something for myself is going to mess with my head and try to stop me doing it. I can't wait for the guilt to no longer be there before I can take care of myself. I will feel the guilt and do it anyway.
Meaning and purpose (made up of contribution, mastery or achievement of a goal)	
Contribution	I want to have a strong connection with my kids, and I don't want to take my frustrations out on them. They are not getting the best version of me. They need a mother who is calmer, more nurturing and energetic. They will not remember if they got to their activities on time, but they will remember how I made them feel.

Mastery	I will develop mastery through: • letting go of certain things, and realising that sometimes 80 per cent or even 60 per cent is good enough • not tying my self-worth and value to the state of our home, how well dressed my kids are, or if I have a cleared out inbox • being able to calm myself and be present with the children; when I am with them, I won't run through all the things I have to do but will instead enjoy the moment.
Courage	Putting firmer boundaries in place will take courage. My kids are going to have to drop some activities and I need my husband to step up and be more involved and hands on. I am going to write a list of what each person is going to help me with. Each week I will find the courage to do something for me that makes me feel alive and energised.

Unhealthy dad strive

The current situation	I am a busy working dad and I have let my health slip. I am not exercising and I have put on lots of weight. I feel lethargic and think I look like shit.
The strive	I want to have my old energy back and be active with the kids. I want to feel good about my appearance and stop worrying about if my health is going to get really bad and if I will have a heart attack. I want to lose 20 kilograms and be at the weight I was before I got married. I have a school reunion in 11 months and I want to do it by then. That is the big achievement. What I really want to achieve is to be consistent and stick to the plan. I know what I have to do with my food and my exercise, and I want to execute on the plan and not get taken off track. I also want to do a 10-kilometre fun run in 12 months' time.

The struggle	• I have tried this in the past. I see good results straightaway but as they slow down I get disheartened and quit. • I am a comfort eater; when I have a hard day, I come home and pig out. Also I use alcohol to numb out at the end of the day. Actually, I drink way too much alcohol and use it to wind down at the end of every day.

How to embrace the struggle and see it as development

Acceptance	I am going to have good days and bad days. I am going to want to quit and I am going to lack motivation. The little voices in my head will try to sabotage my efforts.

Meaning and purpose (made up of contribution, mastery or achievement of a goal)

Contribution	I want to be the active dad and set an example for my kids around the importance of a healthy lifestyle. Plus, I am an older dad because we had kids late, and I want to be around for as long as possible to see my kids grow up and have a family of their own. I want to be mobile in my older age and not a burden on them.
Mastery	I want to master the ability to not let my emotions and negative thoughts take me off course. I want to be able to sit with the discomfort (getting out of bed to exercise, saying no to alcohol or food that is not in my plan). Actually, what I really want to master is the ability to not overthink things. When the alarm goes off at 5.30 am, I lie there for 20 minutes debating whether or not I should get out of bed: 'Will it be cold? Is my bag packed? Will the gym be busy? Will I get a park?' I do my head in and end up just staying in bed. I want to be able to quiet the noise, accept the discomfort and act. If I could master that, it would change my life.

Achievement	I want to achieve the following: • lose 20 kilograms by the school reunion • go to the reunion feeling good about my appearance • run 10 kilometres without thinking I am going to die.
Courage	I will show the courage to say to my mates, clients or co-workers that I am not drinking tonight. (I am surrounded by a lot of big drinkers.) Or that I am only having two drinks. I will have the courage to sit with my negative emotions and accept them rather than chasing them away with food or alcohol.

CAMP QUALITY STRIVE

When you are writing a book, you get hit with insights or inspiration at the most unlikely moments. This one just came to me — at 6.30 am on a Saturday morning. Ordinarily I would be on my way home from my usual 5:30 am gym session at this hour, but I skipped it because my gorgeous six-year-old daughter, Lexie, was not well overnight and she slept next to me. Unfortunately, she likes to kick in her sleep and I have served as a human piñata all night.

As I was lying there, I had a thought. My time as a Camp Quality companion encapsulated striving perfectly. The reason I bring up Camp Quality again is that it was one of the most formative experiences I have ever had. Much development came from that experience, but also a boatload of struggle — oh my gosh, so much struggle. The struggle ranged from fitting the two-week camps into my busy life to sitting with and supporting a family who had just lost their child. Indeed, so much struggle that at many points, friends, girlfriends, parents and loved ones asked me why I was putting myself through the difficult experience.

Here's why.

The strive	I wanted be a consistent companion who attended both the summer and winter camps as well as each year's professional development training. I also wanted to be a supportive, fun and compassionate companion who not only supported the kids but also their families and the other companions who might struggle from time to time.
The struggle	When I started, I was a 21-year-old male who had never really been around loss or grief, and I wasn't particularly good at handling strong emotions. I was going to be around death and loss and sadness like I had never experienced. The biggest struggle was being around the greatest injustice in life — a child dying.

How to embrace the struggle and see it as development

Acceptance	At many moments, I will experience more difficulty and discomfort than I have ever gone through. I am in unchartered territory and, as a result, will freak out from time to time. I will go through sadness, grief and despair. Also, I will have the thoughts such as, *I don't need this in my life, I should quit.* All this discomfort is an opportunity to grow and evolve.

Meaning and purpose (made up of contribution, mastery or achievement of a goal)

Contribution	This one was easy. The experience offered huge opportunities to give back. I wanted to help out those in need any way I could. I wanted to give those parents and siblings who were looking after a child with cancer a break and have some time back. Also I wanted those kids who were gravely ill, some of whom were terminal, to forget about what they are going through for a week and just have the time of their life.

Mastery	I had so many opportunities to develop and master new skills. I had never looked after kids in the past and had many surprises. Holy crap! How long do they take to get ready? And when they finally do get ready, the mess they leave behind is staggering. I learned how to talk to and manage kids in a way that meant they did what I asked them to do. And I learned to manage my own frustration and to display compassion when they were driving me nuts.
Achievement	Each year, I want to attend each summer and winter camp and do at least one training day per year. I want to get my ten-year service badge.
Courage	The courage it takes to be with a family when their child is dying or has died is immense. You just want to run away from that situation. Also it takes courage to go back to being a companion after the eight-year-old boy you looked after for four years has died and everything about camp reminds you of them, and the moments where you turn around and expect them to be there, or when you forget that they are gone and you look for them in a crowd are some sort of cosmic punch in the guts. Even as I write this, I think, *How the hell did I do that?* Like, seriously, how did I do that? I myself marvel at that effort. I have a great level of pride in that.

For me, the camp process was striving in its purest form. It had ups and downs and setbacks and pain, and often I was so deep in the trenches that I couldn't see any light. However, it was an experience that led to more development than anything I have ever done.

And now I have to go — my six year old just woke up and is calling for her piñata.

SUMMARY

- Telling people to have a logical response to struggle is ridiculous. Asking people who are in the midst of challenge to simply have practical or positive thoughts will not work because we are emotional creatures not rational ones.

- The key to seeing struggle as an opportunity to develop is:

  - Accept that struggle is uncomfortable, and it's going to suck. Don't see the discomfort as a reason for not engaging in it. Also accept your reaction to the struggle without judgement. Good, bad, positive or negative, when you accept your reaction to struggle you have a much more constructive response to the struggle.

  - Connect to the meaning and purpose that sits on the other side of that struggle. Meaning and purpose can exist in the achievement of a goal, mastery of a skill and contribution to other people.

  - Focus on and observe how you are being courageous in the struggle.

CHAPTER 9

Striving effectively: background behaviours

In addition to the foreground behaviours covered in the previous chapter, our research showed that strivers also had background behaviours that allowed them to handle struggle much more effectively. Think of these background behaviours as bedrock behaviours—they build a solid foundation on which you can more effectively deal with discomfort.

The five background behaviours are having a clear mental focus, being grateful, connecting with others, taking time to recover and celebrating your victories.

Have a clear mental focus

As outlined in the previous chapter, in order to handle struggle more effectively when you get in the trenches with it, you must accept that it is going to be uncomfortable and accept whatever thoughts and emotions come up for you, focus on the meaning and purpose that sits on the other side of it, and bear witness to your own courage. To do all of these things, you must be able to control your attention and be mindful while dealing with struggle.

In chapter 7, I talk about one of my research studies where we examined a client-facing division of a large financial institution.

At this company, employees were divided into four levels of performance (diamond, gold, silver and bronze). As well as the findings already discussed, my teams and I also found that one of the key characteristics of the high performers that allowed them to deal with struggle so well was their capacity to be focused and present (as shown in the following figure).

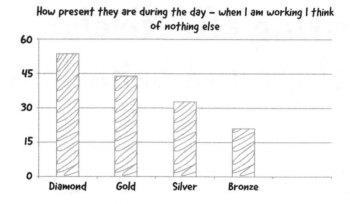

How present they are during the day — when I am working I think of nothing else

Over the past 15 years, mindfulness has experienced a huge surge in popularity. Mindfulness is defined as a state where our attention is fully engaged in what's happening in that present moment. It's also known as 'being present' or 'living in the moment'—whether that is paying complete attention to someone when you are talking to them or being totally immersed in a novel.

Even with this surge in mindfulness awareness, current research suggests that we are losing the ability to be mindful. You don't even have to look at the research for this one—just go outside and observe people anywhere. Go into a restaurant and see people being distracted from those they're dining with by their devices. Or sit in on any meeting, in any company, anywhere in the world and watch attendees focus on their laptops or their phones rather than those in the room. In fact, our attention spans are getting so poor that psychologists have termed a condition called 'continual partial attention' or CPA. This condition captures the idea that rarely is our attention focused on one thing. The common state for people today is for our attention to be spread across a number of things, meaning we are no longer living in the present moment.

Studies show that a scattered, distracted mind leads to:

- increased anxiety levels
- poor attention spans
- higher levels of tiredness and fatigue
- greater chance of burn out
- less connection with the people around us
- reduced performance and efficiency
- poor mental health
- poor decision making
- less enjoyment from life.

The multitasking myth

Before I get into the specifics of how you can improve your mental focus, I first need to clear up an urban myth. Can humans really multitask?

For too long people have prided themselves on being able to multitask. No doubt you've heard (perhaps even made) statements like, 'I am efficient because I can multitask' or 'To do this role effectively, you need to be a multitasker'. However, neuroscience shows that it is impossible for the brain to do two tasks that require attention at the same time. (We can do two things at once as long as one of them does not require attention, such as walking and talking on the phone, where you are not thinking about walking.) When you are doing what everyone considers to be multitasking, what you are actually doing is 'switch-tasking'—where you are switching your attention from one task to another, quickly. This is very stressful for the brain and exhausts it. In fact, a study from Kings College in London compared the cognitive ability of people who had been multitasking all day with people who were … wait for it … stoned and discovered the stoned people outperformed the multitasking people on everything they were given.

Let me prove it to you! Write the statement, 'Multitasking disengages my brain', but write one letter of the statement only and then below it write the first letter of the alphabet, then write the next letter of the statement and then the next letter of the alphabet. Continue writing one letter of the statement followed by the next letter of the alphabet until it looks like the following:

m u l t i t a s k i n g d i s e n g a g e s m y b r a i n
a b c d e f g h i j k l m n o p q r s t u v w x y z a b c

Note down the time this takes you.

Repeat the exercise again, but this time write the statement in full and then the letters of the alphabet underneath in full. Note down the time this takes you.

What you will find is that the first method will take you four to five times longer than the second method.

In the first method, you are multitasking it (swapping your focus from one task to the next), while in the second method you are completing one task before moving on to the next one. When we shift our attention from one task to another we experience something called an 'attentional blink'. This is where the brain is resetting what it is focusing on and, at this point, cannot take in information or recall information. This is the reason multitasking makes you so slow. People think they are being super-efficient when they multitask; however, they are actually being ineffective and stressing their brain.

> **People think they are being super-efficient when they multitask; however, they are actually being ineffective and stressing their brain.**

The benefits of better mental focus

Having better mental focus means you are much more likely to apply the three foreground strategies (covered in the previous chapter) to struggle. However, other benefits that come from clear mental focus are:

- reduced anxiety
- higher energy levels
- greater levels of happiness
- improved cognition—you can take in more information, think more clearly and thus make better decisions
- higher levels of creativity and innovation
- much higher productivity
- more enjoyment from experiences.

Being present and focused also develops and deepens relationships with other people. You may have heard that the greatest compliment you can give another human being is your undivided attention, yet we rarely do it. A study in Sweden showed a manager not being present with a team increased a team member's chance of being disengaged by 44 per cent. They showed that if the manager was present but critical of their team, the chance of disengagement was 21 per cent (which means you can be a jerk, just as long as you are a present jerk). However, if the manager is present with them and complimented them on their work, they became much more engaged.

So how do we become more focused?

One of the greatest things about my job is that at conferences I get to meet the most wildly successful and interesting people. At one conference dinner I was sitting with a group of neuroscientists who study the impact of mindfulness on the brain. After three glasses of red (okay, I am a cheap date), I said to them, 'Mindfulness kind of gives me the shits. It's so esoteric and vague. How do I make it more tangible? Actually, is there a formula to being more mindful? How do I do mindfulness?'

Now, they were ahead of me and most of them had had five glasses of red wine so they were feeling pretty loose. One of them grabbed a napkin and a pen and said, 'You want the formula? Here's the formula!' He then proceeded to write down the following six-step formula to being more focused:

1. Every day do 5 to 15 minutes of formal attention training, such as meditation or relaxation. The best thing to do is download a relaxation app on your phone and do it each day.

2. Pick a series of tasks that you want to be completely present during. When you do these tasks, focus on being immersed in each part of the task. Some examples of what you can choose are:

   - eating
   - brushing teeth
   - reading
   - exercise
   - weekly team meeting (no phone or email).

3. Choose a series of people who you will endeavour to be completely present with—for example, children, partner, friends when socialising, the people you manage and peers at work. Put your phone away and be present.

4. Get a hobby that requires attention, such as music, reading, art, chess, drawing, cooking, learning a language, golf, singing, a team sport, taxidermy (just kidding, that's creepy). Being immersed in a hobby retrains your brain to be present.

5. Have device-free time every single day. One thing I've implemented with great success is putting my phone away when I come home from work. It allows me to be far more

present, far more engaged and a far better dad and husband. Actively seek out and factor in time away from your devices. The impact on your attention and anxiety levels will be profound. In fact, a recent study in the United States had people sit in a room by themselves and complete a difficult task, with different groups dealing with varying levels of distraction. They then measured mistake rates. The first group, which had no distractions of any kind, made a few mistakes due to the difficult nature of the task. The second group had their phones with them and the researchers sent them messages to interrupt them during the task. For this group, mistake rates skyrocketed. I mean, they were through the roof. The interruptions destroyed their performance of the task. The third group was the most interesting of all. They had their phones with them but received no messages or specific interruptions. The result of just having the phone on the desk in front of them, however, still dramatically increased their mistake rate.

6. Observe your attention during the day, and endeavour to be present with each thing you do. If you notice your attention has drifted, re-focus and bring it back to what you are doing. Studies show that attention is like a muscle and the more you practise it, the better it gets. Endeavour to go through your day in a more focused state.

Be grateful, God damn it!!

Another background behaviour that we found built a strong platform from which people could more effectively handle struggle was high levels of gratitude. This was an observed finding that ran through all our different research projects. People who were strong at striving were also really high on their levels of gratitude.

This finding is supported by other studies in this area. Professor Todd Kashdan's study showed that in Vietnam War veterans, being grateful helped reduce the negative impacts of post-traumatic stress disorder. (Todd published the findings of his study under the slightly academic title, 'Gratitude and hedonic and eudaimonic well-being in Vietnam War veterans'.) And in 'What good are positive emotions in crises?' Barbara Fredrickson outlines that for people affected by the September 11 terrorist attacks, gratitude increased their level of resilience and protected them against depression.

So being grateful helps you deal with struggle, but lots of research from the past ten years shows that actively being grateful also boosts your wellbeing, quality of sleep, empathy for others and self-esteem.

This paired with my team's observation that strivers are high in gratitude tells me that this is a critical background behaviour to help people deal with struggle. For the best results, reflect on gratitude between daily and once a week—somewhere in that range seems to be the sweet spot, according to the research. Focus on what you are grateful for in your life, big and small. And you can incorporate a gratitude practice into your life in many ways. One of the best is, if you have a family or partner, to do it around the dinner table. This is a brilliant practice to get into. You could also practise gratitude in the transition home, during your meditative practice or as part of any journalling you do.

Connect with others: high struggle needs high support

Without doubt, one of the most important background behaviours is having strong connections with the people around you. The three areas that my team and I found this mattered the most in were:

- supervisor or leader support at work

- peer support at work

- support in your personal life from friends, family and/or partner.

This was such a strong finding. When you have rock-solid support around you, there is very little struggle that you can't take on. Support in these three areas dramatically improved people's capacity to strive.

> When you have rock-solid support around you, there is very little struggle that you can't take on.

Here is one example. In one of my team's studies, we explored one of the toughest business environments you will ever come across: a contact centre. But this was no ordinary contact centre; this was a contact centre within the collections department of a bank.

(Was that an audible gasp from you?)

Employees at this contact centre spend their day chasing irresponsible people for repayments or, as a final straw, telling these people their stuff is about to be taken away. Or so I thought. I went into this environment believing they were dealing with irresponsible and frivolous people who simply got in over their heads and couldn't pay their bills. But that's not the case. The contact centre employees often deal with people who are victims of violence, people who have gravely sick children and have had to stop work to take care of them, and people with mental health issues battling their own demons. This is an incredibly tough and frequently emotionally draining job.

I got to know this group on a deep level and developed a tremendous amount of respect for them, because they genuinely cared and wanted the best for their customers. Rather than just taking their stuff away, staff in the contact centre worked with people to try to get their repayment schedule back on track. We did both a research project and a training intervention with them. At the start of our research, we examined the factors that drove high performance in this environment and allowed people not to buckle under the significant emotional struggle that comes with the job. Two clear factors stood out:

1. *Having a strong connection with their leader.* This was demonstrated through statements such as:

    -   'I feel comfortable discussing my personal or family issues with my people leader.'

    -   'My people leader demonstrates care for me and my team.'

    -   'My people leader gives me helpful feedback about my performance.'

2. *Feeling they were part of a community at work.* This was demonstrated through statements such as:

    -   'I have the opportunity to develop close friendships in my job.'

    -   'I have the opportunity to socialise with others in my work.'

    -   'People I work with take a personal interest in me.'

What we learned from this group was that their capacity to strive forward was built on a strong platform of support.

To draw on another example, I only need to look to The Flourish Movement, which, I know, I've already mentioned a few times—because I have totally fallen in love with the school leaders and the work we do with them. The results of this project have been staggering, with school leaders reporting they were more efficient and more focused after the program, leading to them being able to focus more on the things that make the school better and getting better student outcomes. School leaders also reported they were able to spend more time with their families and looking after themselves. Best of all, they felt they were a better version of themselves after completing the program, and that the culture at their school had improved. (For the full outcomes in these areas, go to www.dradamfraser.com/doe-report and click the link to see the latest results.)

I have spent a lot of time trying to understand the factors that are driving the success of this program. One of the biggest factors I have uncovered is the connection and support that grows within the group. We keep our groups small (25 to 30 people) and in the same geographical location to build connection. We then purposefully drive this connection by slowly building trust through vulnerability. Another way to describe this is we get them to take off the mask, leave it at the door and show up as their real selves.

This is an experience school leaders rarely get, because the majority of their training focuses on systems and compliance and how they can help support other people (including staff, parents and students). Ours is the first large-scale program that we know of that is totally focused on school leaders' wellbeing. Many participants talk about never before being as honest or vulnerable with other school leaders, and how freeing it is. Some of the school leaders say just knowing that other participants share the same fears, concerns and insecurities is transformational for them.

One of the biggest blocks to school leaders' wellbeing is their guilt about taking time for themselves. However, when they get the permission and support of their peers to do this, they finally begin to put themselves higher on the priority list.

Another strategy we implemented was to create buddy pairs in the program, where each pair spoke once a week to check in and hold each other accountable for their action plans. Initially, many of the school leaders saw this as another task to do. But they quickly fell in love with the process. Talking each week with a trusted peer who you can bounce ideas off, share your victories with and vent your frustrations to is good for the soul. Many of them enjoyed the process so much that after finishing the program they were still talking to their buddies every week 18 months on. To illustrate this, here's some feedback I received from participant Jason Ezzy:

> Twelve months on from our commencement of Flourish, I wanted to share some feedback. We were just reflecting on how our group of principals feels even more connected than ever before. We meet for informal catch-ups semi-regularly and check in on each other when we know that people have things going on. A measure of this is that we have 57 of the 63 principals in our networks registered to come along to our annual conference. Our usual attendance is around 40. This is phenomenal and I believe directly linked to the stronger connections through our flourish journey.

The most moving story by far from the Flourish Movement occurred when one of our school leaders went through the tragic and sudden death of a staff member who also happened to be one of her closest friends. It was just before the state principals' conference, which she loved to attend. She had decided because of the circumstances not to attend the conference. However, her staff literally ran an intervention and insisted that she go because they felt she needed it. When she reached her room at the conference hotel and was about to open the door to enter, she heard voices on the other side. She went back down to the front desk and told them they'd mistakenly given her the wrong room, because someone was already in that room. She was assured it was the right room so went back upstairs, slowly opened the door, put her head in and said, 'Hello?'—to be greeted by her Flourish group.

They said to her, 'We heard what happened and we just want to let you know that we're here for you'.

Don't see connecting with people as an inconvenience; see it as investing in your and their wellbeing, performance and capacity to handle struggle.

In this busy, fast-paced, demanding digital world, we spend far too much time with machines and screens. I implore you: spend more time connecting with the people around you. Don't see connecting with people as an inconvenience; see it as investing in your and their wellbeing, performance and capacity to handle struggle. You no doubt know the importance of connecting to those who mean the most to you in your personal life, but also ensure that you spend time connecting to people on a deep level at work.

Talking to your team on a deep personal level

Over the past couple years, we have been trialling a new model to deliver wellbeing programs en masse in organisations. Our research showed that most large-scale wellbeing programs are delivered through an online medium. The downside of this is that most of these programs sit idly by, unused. For about a year, I have obsessed about how to make online wellbeing programs capture people's attention. Finally I solved the puzzle, through realising that the problem with wellbeing programs is that they only focus on wellbeing.

In a world where margins and budgets are so tight and our time is so precious, I realised that wellbeing programs need to achieve far more than an improvement in wellbeing. With the help of my team, I came up with a model that used wellbeing programs to improve team trust, connection, culture, engagement and leadership capability—oh, and of course wellbeing.

Now I'm not going to reveal the specifics of this model because we are in the process of trademarking it. What I can say is that it involves leaders building their facilitation and coaching skills by leading their teams through parts of the program. Through this process, leaders are helped to have deep conversations with their team that revolve around themes such as:

- Where do you find meaning and purpose in your role?
- How are you dealing with the stress of the job?
- Are you happy with the impact you're having on your family when you get home at the end of the day?
- What are the doubts you have about your capability?

And our data is showing that having these types of conversations creates an explosion of trust through a team.

We examined the impact of leaders going through this model with their teams in a recent study. We compared leaders in the study who did the program with their teams to leaders who chose not to participate in the process. (Don't you hate having to make things voluntary and not being able to force people into it?) Individuals in teams with a leader who went through the program with them saw the following benefits above individuals in a team with a leader who did not engage in the program:

- 49 per cent greater level of implementation of the program into their daily habits

- 73.8 per cent improvement in the culture of their team

- 160 per cent increase in how supportive they thought their leader was

- 43.4 per cent decrease in their stress levels at work.

When we interviewed the leaders who engaged in the program, the most common piece of feedback was along the lines of, 'Through having those deep conversations I learned more about my team in that program than I have in the last four years'. Connection is king.

My final word on this: our research showed that what builds connection the most is when you are vulnerable, honest and authentic with another person.

Take time to recover

The next background behaviour is the art of self-care. This is a huge one. If you are going to strive and embrace struggle, you need to spend time on recovery. You have to nurture yourself and invest in self-care. When you get in the trenches with struggle, you come out with bumps and bruises and sometimes drained energy. Therefore, you need to re-energise so you can keep striving forward. If you spend too much time in striving without self-care, you will burn out.

This may be controversial and I hate to generalise but our research showed that, compared to men, women find self-care very difficult. Society has sold them on this bullshit story that taking time for yourself is being selfish or self-indulgent. Many have bought into the lie that women have to:

- do it all

- do it perfectly

- not let anyone see you not cope.

Be perfect, be amazing, look after everyone and, for the love of God, don't show any cracks.

I only have one piece of advice on self-care, and it relates to the acceptance step I discussed in the previous chapter: *Don't wait for the guilt to go before you practise self-care.* Guilt will always be there, so don't wait for the guilt to go before you start looking after yourself (because otherwise you will be waiting a very long time).

Self-care is a very personal thing; what works for you may not work for someone else. Go with what works for you. There are no hard or fast rules, but I can give you some guidance. From our studies, we found that self-care functions on three levels.

Level 1: Each day, calm your mind

This practice has a lot of parallels with the first background behaviour of being present. Shutting down your mind and relaxing your nervous system is a vital way to practise self-care. Today most people's minds are so busy they can never truly relax. Have you ever gone on holidays and realised it takes a week for your mind to unwind? Yeah! Most of us have lost the capacity for our brains to calm down. But we can change that.

Activities that help our mind calm down include listening to a relaxation app on your phone, counting while you breathe in a relaxed way, reading a fiction book with relaxing music in the background, and meditation. (Reading fiction is particularly good if you can't get into meditation. Insert small moments of reading into your day.) The bad news is that TV does not fit into this. TV is a very passive medium, meaning it doesn't require a lot of attention. Because of this while you are watching TV your attention tends to drift and usually ends up in worry and concern (usually about all the things you have to do), which creates more stress. Also the majority of people watching TV are interacting with another screen, such as their phone or their laptop where they are clearing out emails.

So don't turn on the TV straightaway. Instead, every day aim to spend five to ten minutes in some sort of activity that puts you in a deep state of relaxation. My team's research shows that even this small amount gives you a huge benefit. These short bursts of relaxation build on each other like compound interest, and you are better off doing a short burst each day than larger bursts infrequently.

Many people we studied said when they try to do these activities, after about two minutes their brain starts shouting something like, 'YOU HAVE SHIT TO DO!!' and they abandon their efforts. This is normal. It's ironic but people obsess and stress about getting their relaxation right. Do the activity rather than judging your performance. The key is to develop a consistent habit of calming your mind.

Level 2: Insert some bright spots into your week

Self-care is not just about winding down; it's also about winding up. This level is around filling up your cup. We spend so much time giving to other people—to our team at work, our clients, our families, our friends, our community—but neglect to think about what we do to fill ourselves back up. What are the things that re-energise you? What inspires you? What fills your bucket?

Each week, build in a ritual that feeds your soul. This layer in particular is deeply personal, but examples from our studies included taking up a hobby such as art or music. One professional in particular said he used to get together with his mates to play music in their band on a Tuesday night. But when he got a promotion, he decided he was too busy for that so he stopped. Following one of our programs he decided to add this back in. Next time I saw him he said, 'Why did I ever stop doing it? Taking that short time to do that activity feeds my soul and makes me a better leader, parent, husband. It put a smile back on my face'.

Other ideas are

- a yoga class
- getting a massage
- singing in a choir
- going for a bike ride Sunday morning with your friends then catching up over breakfast
- being in nature
- visiting the beach.

The possibilities are endless, so spend some time finding out what lights you up. Mine is a little unusual (not 'I wear women's shoes' unusual). On a Sunday morning, I wake up at 5.50 am. I am in my car by 6 am and driving to Shelly Beach near Manly. Then I swim from Shelly beach to Manly beach and back. Then I have a coffee at the Bower café while I look at one of the best views on the planet. Then I drive home, arrive by around 9 am and have breakfast with my family (armed with a coffee for my Italian wife, of course). I am not sure if it is the drive, or the swim, or the quiet time, but something about this ritual fills my soul like there is no tomorrow. It is so special to me I even do it in winter. I put up with the cold water (I hate the cold—like, really hate the cold) and the fact that it takes 45 minutes for my feet to no longer be numb. And when I miss it, I notice a visible decline in my mood.

Remember to fill your cup each week.

Level 3: Have a day of no responsibility

Once a month, aim to have a day that has zero level of responsibility—a day where you have no plans, no agenda and no-one to look after. You can do whatever the hell you feel like. This level focuses on removing responsibility and inserting freedom. Our lives are so scheduled and we have so many things that we're responsible for. This modern, fast-paced life wears us down. In my house, the level of planning needed to co-ordinate two parents with busy jobs, one who travels a lot for work, two kids with multiple activities, a dog and a social life, would rival a special forces unit planning a mission.

To combat your own busyness and planning, spend time in a state where you don't have an agenda, no schedule whatsoever, where you are not responsible for another human being, you don't have to achieve any specific outcome, and have no time pressure at all. This is called freedom. Aim to get one day of no responsibility each month. Our studies show that days like this are incredibly restorative.

Before you head off, here are some things to consider with this day. Most people have to do it on the weekend but you get extra points for doing it mid-week. Watching other people go to work can be incredibly restorative. In a lot of our research we asked people to spend this day on their own, but you can spend it with other people—as long as you stick to the rules of no agenda, no tasks that you need to achieve and no responsibility.

As I write this, I am in the planning phase of a deep analysis project, focusing on burnout in women. Already, our initial analysis and research has uncovered something quite fascinating. One of the things that exhausts women the most is planning stress. Some evidence suggests that in heterosexual relationships men have become more involved and helpful in the home. However, our interviews with women reveal that while men are more involved in the work, almost always it is the female in the relationship who co-ordinates and organises everything. Many highlighted points such as, 'I still do all the planning. I own all the tasks. I co-ordinate things and he chimes in and helps out. Even if I am not doing the task, I am still organising it'. In other words, the men are doing what they are told to do by their female partner. They are better at taking delegation orders.

The idea to focus on this area actually came from my wife, who is far brighter than I am. One day she said to me, 'Yeah, you are super helpful around the house and you cook dinner and clean up and do the washing. But I co-ordinate the house—all the kids' activities, the running of the home. While you might do lots of the tasks, the planning still comes down to me and I find it exhausting. The planning load of trying to keep everything running smoothly is huge for me'. This was a very jagged pill for me to swallow because I have always been a husband and dad who saw themselves as being very involved in both the home and parenting. Following this conversation, however, I immediately started to take ownership of things and it massively improved not only my wife's level of burnout but also our connection.

Having said that, it dramatically increased my stress levels. Far out! Planning and co-ordination of the home is freaking exhausting. It drains you! I had to use many of the strategies in this book to cope. How this relates to the day of no responsibility is that the constant planning and co-ordination is draining. A day of no responsibility releases the pressure valve a bit.

TAKING TIME OUT WHEN YOU'RE AT YOUR BUSIEST

I was once asked to do a keynote presentation to the top 30 leaders of the risk division of a major bank. Within this presentation, I talked about the three levels of recovery I've discussed here. Following the presentation, the head of risk for that bank came up and said,

That is really interesting. When I think about preventing burnout I always think of taking a long break such as an extended holiday, I have never thought about doing these small, regular, consistent bursts of recovery.

About two months later I got a call from his EA saying that he was doing a road show around the country, presenting to everyone who worked in risk, and he wanted me to do the same presentation on the prevention of burnout. (Just to give you some context, this group had recently been smashed by the regulator and the risk team had a huge amount of work to do in a very small period of time to make the bank compliant.) We set it up and I joined the road show.

At the first presentation, after I explained the three levels of recovery, he stood up and said, 'Can I just stop you there?' He then walked up on stage and stood next to me. I am thinking, *What the hell is going on here?* In front of the entire group, he said,

When I first heard Adam present this, while I found it interesting, I also thought, *This guy is on drugs. There is no way I have time to do things that fill my cup or take a day to myself. That is impossible.* However, I couldn't stop thinking about it because I am hurting. The work load is huge, I am tired, I feel like I am burning out, I am neglecting my family and the guilt around that is huge for me. Because I was struggling, I tried the first two layers. They worked so well I thought, *I am going for gold.* And I tried the day of no responsibility.

The way I approached it is that I sat down with my wife and outlined what Adam presented to us. I said to my wife, 'I feel like I need that day, but I feel so guilty asking for it'. She looked at me and said, 'I want that day! We can take it in turns. If you get it, I get it too'. We decided that I would go first and my wife took the kids out after breakfast and planned to return at dinner time.

When I asked him on stage how he went, he replied,

I spent the first couple of hours kind of walking around the house. I didn't know what to do with the free time. My life is so organised and scripted I didn't know how to deal with free time. Finally, I thought, *I want to go see that movie.* So I went to the movies on my own, then I went and had lunch, then I went for a walk to the beach, and after that I went home and read a book. I just went wherever the wind took me.

I asked how he felt after that day, and he replied, 'I felt so good I booked the next one in'. He then addressed the group and said,

We have this mountain of work we are trying to climb. We are not even halfway up and I can see that it is having an impact on us. We don't have time to take a holiday or a large break. What we can do is insert these short, regular and consistent moments of recovery. I encourage everyone in this team to try these strategies because they are making a huge difference to me.

The mistake we make around self-care is that it is not some new age, hippy concept. People have been doing this forever, but there is just more need for it today given the rising levels of pressure and expectation. Gee, even my quiet, Scottish, motor mechanic father practised self-care:

- Every day after work, he would go into his shed and tinker with stuff—in other words, he turned his mind off and was present.
- Each week he played in a band—this filled his soul because he was a music tragic.
- He regularly spent Sundays watching golf or car racing on TV, which he almost always fell asleep in front of.

One of the most important background behaviours we can do to help us manage struggle and challenge is spending time on recovery.

Celebrate your victories

The final background behaviour is reflecting on your victories and evolution.

As we discussed in chapter 4 it is important for individuals to focus on progress and evolution, and doing so dramatically increases our capacity to tolerate discomfort.

In this section, I provide steps you can take to spend more time reflecting on evolution. These steps are the result of many projects my team and I have run in this area. They have also been influenced by two friends: Darren Hill and Dr Jason Fox. Apart from inspiring me to dress better, these two have done some deep thinking in this area and helped me crystallise my thoughts and focus. Thanks, boys!

Have clear goals and take action

To reflect on evolution, you must be doing something. The first step is to set yourself (and your team if you are a leader) very clear and specific goals or aspirations, and a clear vision. Develop absolute clarity around what you want to achieve. This can be done on not only a professional level but also a personal one. Too often people have goals at work but not in their personal life. What are your goals for your relationships, your health, your parenting or your stress management, for example?

Reflect on 'being' not just 'doing'

My team and I recently completed some research on high-performing teams and discovered that the common characteristic was that every day they talked about evolution. Interestingly, they discussed progress on two levels:

1. *Doing:* This is where you focus on the things you do, what tasks you completed, what goals were achieved or what key performance indicators (KPIs) you hit.

2. *Being:* This is about the personal traits you are exhibiting. As an individual, are you being courageous, persistent or curious? As a team, are you being resilient, collaborative and innovative? This is about focusing on how the team's culture is evolving and progressing.

Make it visual

Include a really good visual representation of your evolution so it is front of mind and you can see it. Being able to visualise your progress greatly increases your motivation. A mate of mine set a goal to do meditation every single day without fail. To map his progress, he put a red bar on his electronic calendar every day he meditated. He wanted a constant red bar from one day to another. He refers to it as, 'Don't break the red'.

Any visual representation of progress helps with engagement. This is why charities often use the thermometer model (where they colour in a thermometer as the money raises towards their goal) to represent their fundraising efforts.

Get an external perspective

External validation around your evolution carries a huge amount of weight. Whenever you can, get an outsider's view of you or your team's progress. It can really drive motivation.

Make it specific

Whenever you can put metrics around your evolution, have numbers, specific measurements, stories and clear examples of your progress. Always seek tangible evidence to measure your progress.

Make it frequent

Reflect on evolution regularly. A great formula to focus on is 1:7:30:90:365. This means reflect on evolution daily, weekly, monthly, quarterly and annually.

The following table provides an example of how you could use this formula with a work team.

Yearly	This usually occurs at your offsite or annual conference. At this level, focus on the big wins the team have achieved, along with the 'why' of the team and 'why' do you do what you do. Relate that 'why' to the strategic focus of the organisation, the culture of the team, how the culture has evolved, and the traits and characteristics of the team.
Quarterly	At your quarterly meeting, the key focus is activity. Go over how the activity you have completed has got you closer to the annual goal. Another great idea is to invite an external group or person to the meeting — someone you collaborate with or a stakeholder, or even a client. Ask them to present on their own progress and achievements, how the work of your group has enabled that progress, and their perspective on how your team has evolved and improved and made progress.

Monthly	The monthly meeting is really important to motivate and pick the team up. Do this by reflecting on positive progress. The focus here is to be upbeat and enthusiastic to motivate the team. While this depends on logistics, a great way to do the monthly meeting is a long lunch where you go offsite. Go somewhere low-key to reflect on the progress over the month. It is important to be in a different environment. Key points to cover: • significant wins and achievements • how the team is and how they are working together • what progress has been made as a culture. Also include positive stories and examples.
Weekly	The weekly reflection really focuses on key wins that people have had. It also allows people to cover friction points (what is holding back their progress). People in the meeting may be able to give insights and solutions to help that person to improve their progress. If you are geographically dispersed, you may choose to do this via email. Get people to fill out a template that covers their key goals, any significant news, big wins and achievements, plus any critical communication and, importantly, how they are feeling. Really strong research shows that asking staff how they are feeling creates a much stronger team culture.
Daily	A real strong trend in Silicon Valley is daily huddles. This is a 10-minute stand-up meeting where teams quickly share their wins for the day. It is a great way to build enthusiasm, momentum and cohesiveness. In the huddle, people share significant wins from yesterday, their daily activity, top priorities, anything they need help with and key project milestones.

The background or bedrock behaviours can be combined with everything discussed so far to create the following model.

SUMMARY

- The background behaviours create a strong basis from which you can strive. The five behaviours are:

  - Develop strong mental focus — the capacity to be mindful and present dramatically helps people strive and handle struggle.

  - Practise being grateful for what you have — do this regularly (between each day and once a week).

  - Connect with others to build a strong tribe that have your back.

  - Practise recovery — the strive does take it out of you so you have to spend time on recovery and filling up your cup. Do this by calming your brain each day, adding in a weekly bright spot and once a month removing responsibility and an agenda.

  - Take time to celebrate your progress and evolution.

CHAPTER 10

The future of work

Whenever the future of work is discussed, terms like 'artificial intelligence', 'augmented reality', 'virtual reality' and 'machine learning' always seem to be thrown around. And in 2017, a Dell Technologies report documented research on the future of work completed by the Institute for the Future (IFTF). This report claims 45 per cent of the surveyed 4000 senior decision-makers from across the world said they were concerned about becoming obsolete in the next three to five years. Nearly half of the same group said they don't know what their industry would look like in just three years' time. These sentiments have been echoed in Gartner's 'Playbook for the future of work' report, where 73 per cent of executives surveyed believed that changes will occur faster, forcing companies to go through rapid change such as restructure, cultural change, mergers or acquisitions, often simultaneously.

Broad themes in the future of work

My team and I surveyed over 2000 Australian employees, asking them to describe their current working environment. Four themes came out:

1. My job is more complex than it has ever been; I have more stakeholders and more people to consult with.

2. There is more uncertainty than ever before; I am not sure what is coming next. (This could be due to factors such as shifts in technology, changes in regulation and alterations in consumer behaviour.)

3. There is more to do; my role is broader than before, I am responsible for more things and I have more tasks to complete.

4. There is more pace; I have to work faster than I have in the past and there is greater expectation to have things done more rapidly.

These studies show the way we are working today is shifting dramatically. I was recently at a function talking to the Dean of a business school attached to a university. He said, 'I used to teach that change was moving from one steady state to another steady state. Now there is no such thing as a steady state'.

And further research into the future of work, such as that completed by Boston Consulting Group and Deloitte, is also seeing similar themes emerge.

The first of these themes is human and machine partnerships. This is where people and machines integrate to achieve optimal outcomes—whether that is in the context of work–life balance, health, efficiency at work, tapping into available resources or leveraging data analytics.

The second is the 'gig economy'. This is where workers of the future will not own a job but rather will possess a skill set that will be used on a project basis. Rather than having full-time employment, people will work on specific pieces of work.

The third is 'in the moment learning'. Rather than traditional providers of learning, such as universities, technical schools or training programs, workers in the future will use augmented and virtual reality to be fed the information that they need in real-time so they can learn on the job.

Struggle and strive in the future

These three themes are merely people's prediction of what the future will be. It's hard to say with any certainty what exactly the future of work will look like, but we do know that it will be vastly different. Because of this, a lot more ambiguity, complexity, uncertainty and rapid-scale change will emerge in our work. A constant bedfellow of these four things is a shed-load of struggle and challenge. Whenever we go through transformation, we experience a huge amount of discomfort. As a result, we are going to find ourselves in the strive zone much more often.

From my experience, the average employee is terrified by digital disruption, fearing that digital is going to change everything, that they won't have the skills to interact with it and it will take away their jobs. As a result, they resist digital transformation. What this tells us is that now, more than ever before, we need to help the workforce of the future develop a far more functional and constructive relationship with discomfort and struggle. Everything I've been discussing in this book is critical for any organisation moving forward. We need to help employees move from struggle to strive.

Within this, I am seeing a group of leaders who are trying to provide certainty to their people but can't. They are like over-protective parents not wanting their kids to be uncomfortable. You can't say to people, 'Okay, we have gone through a restructure, but it will now return to normal and we will slot into business as usual'. The waves of change keep hitting us like a never-ending tsunami. Rather than leaders trying to make the discomfort go away, they need to support their people through the discomfort and facilitate them into the striving process.

> **One of the most critical roles of leaders, now and in the future, is to coach and support their people to see the struggle as an opportunity to develop, not as a threat.**

One of the most critical roles of leaders, now and in the future, is to coach and support their people to see the struggle as an opportunity to develop, not as a threat. Moving your team from 'threat' to 'development' creates a colossal shift in performance.

STRIVING INTO THE FUTURE

Lee-Anne Carson helps organisations transition into the future of work. She has an amazing history of high-level HR roles in various organisations and so is well positioned to give insight into the work force of the future. She told me,

First of all, we have to stop calling it the 'future of work', because it is here and now. Calling it the future of work makes people complacent and lets them develop the attitude of it's not their problem. Leaders are thinking it won't happen on their watch. In fact, many organisations are playing down how much change is happening right now because they don't want to panic their workforce and see fear propagated around their employees. In my work, I see people who are incredibly anxious and fearful of the changes that are affecting them. People are extremely concerned for their jobs. They worry, 'Am I adding value now and will I be employable moving into the future?'

Most people are acting out of fear for themselves, fear for the future, fear for their teams, fear for their organisation and fear for the economy. In particular, leaders are really struggling with taking their teams from the known to the unknown. As leaders, we have to understand our own anxieties and know that our people are feeling the same.

To manage this, there has to be a transparency in our communication and a conversation that we are going to do this together and that we will stand beside each other and tackle it together. The successful worker and leader of the future is going to have to be okay with uncertainty and ambiguity, and help support the people they work with or lead to be okay with it as well.

After I shared our research with her, Lee-Anne commented,

If we stay in fear, we will be passed by. Jobs will go too and organisations are interested in people who will drive the evolution not be a drag on it. People who can see struggle as an opportunity to develop will be okay in the world of work. If you struggle, learn, accomplish — and struggle, learn, accomplish again — you widen your opportunity for the future of work.

Again, our inability to sit with discomfort is blocking our ability to evolve with the future of work.

Another expert in this area is Allison Keogh, a well-respected leadership consultant and coach throughout Asia–Pacific, and one of the smartest people I know. She told me,

> Due to our obsession of only working in our strengths, I am walking into environments where people won't do things they are not good at. They constantly stay within their comfort zone and will not take on things they are not comfortable with. This obviously limits their learning. People are using their strengths profile as an excuse to avoid work that makes them uncomfortable. The fallout of too much attention on strengths is a pervasive attitude in the workforce of, 'I'm not good at that so I won't do it'. If we stick in our strengths for too long, our learning becomes narrower, and narrower.

One of the great points Allison made was that often what people are good at or feel comfortable with is not what the organisation needs.

> In an ideal world it would be great for every project you work on to match your personal passions, but we don't always have that opportunity. Sometimes what an individual wants to do doesn't align to the organisation's strategy. In that case, that person needs to sit with that discomfort, see it as an opportunity to develop and learn and action it, because it serves the greater good.

I see a similar focus with development plans, where we over emphasise people tapping into their personal aspirations and passions for their career development, even where these are not aligned to the strategic objectives of the organisation. I hear people say comments like, 'I don't want to do work that doesn't align to my personal passions and what I like doing'. People are missing out on so much growth because they are stuck in the mentality of focusing on what they are good at and what they like. As I have highlighted throughout the book, my team's research is showing dramatic benefits of doing things that you are not good at and that you don't like.

We have gone too far in our leadership development of tapping into people's strengths and passions. Of course, asking people to use their strengths and connecting them to passion is a great strategy. However, it shouldn't be absolute. We can't develop to our potential if we stay in this very small lane of only working in our strengths and passions.

And this will only become more important. The capacity to strive through struggle and discomfort is one of the critical skills all employees will need into the future.

SUMMARY

- We are in a period of disruption and change that is making our heads spin.

- Some of the popular predictions for the future of work are:

  - human and machine partnerships increasing

  - fewer people having a 'job' and more people working on a project basis

  - learning occurring more in the moment rather than being course-based.

- In all honesty, we can't accurately predict what the future of work will look like, but we know it will be different, and that change will create a great deal of discomfort for people.

- The experts I interviewed said they had observed that people's fear and anxiety around the future of work are causing them to resist the changes and not evolve.

- Having a striving response to the changing world is a critical step forward for organisations.

- Leaders can't give their teams certainty about the future, but they can stand shoulder to shoulder with their teams, facing the future together.

CHAPTER 11

Helping others strive

Striving should not be all about you. At many points of your life, you are going to have people around you who are striving and, of course, they will get their arse kicked by struggle. At this point, you want to support them in the process. This not only helps them evolve and become a better version of themselves but also provides an amazing opportunity to develop an incredible bond with them. Supporting people who are in the trenches with struggle builds deep, deep connection.

Supporting others in their strive

The striving support process is made up of a few different considerations, and I discuss these over the next sections.

Stop rescuing people

A key mindset is to stop trying to rescue people from struggle and challenge. One of the things that blocks people's development is that we won't allow them to sit with discomfort. When we see people we care about get into the trenches with discomfort our natural instinct is to want to make them feel better and fix the situation. However, this robs them of the opportunity to be courageous and evolve.

I frequently see this in leaders. When their team come to them with a problem, the narrative they have in their head is along the lines of, 'If I am a good leader, I will solve this for them', and 'Leaders should have all the answers'. As a result, they solve the issue for them. The staff member is ecstatic because the struggle has been taken care of. But the leader will then complain that their team members don't think for themselves and they are always interrupting them to ask dumb questions. While they are complaining, the leader's rescuing is reinforcing this behavioural loop. What they are far better doing is letting the staff member sit with the struggle by having a coaching response—that is, asking them questions and getting them to come up with solutions. This response enables the team member to evolve and strive.

Rescuing is especially evident with parents when they will not let their children embrace struggle. Like with the team member, a rescuing response from parents holds their children back from developing and puts them in a learnt helplessness mindset.

> **A rescuing response from parents holds their children back from developing and puts them in a learnt helplessness mindset.**

Obviously, in some situations we need to intervene and help people—for example, if someone is going through abuse or being bullied or in a situation where they have no hope of pulling themselves out, we want to help them. Ask yourself: am I rescuing them and robbing them of an opportunity to develop?

Show empathy and validation

One of the most critical aspects of supporting people through struggle is displaying empathy and validating how they feel when in discomfort. Acknowledge that their situation is difficult and uncomfortable. Also validate the thoughts, feelings, sensations and behaviours they have around it. Don't brush off their challenge as insignificant. Nothing is worse than when you are feeling swamped and your leader acts as if you are overreacting. When people are deep in struggle, always validate what they are thinking and feeling. This strategy relates heavily to the acceptance piece in the forground behaviours chapter. The only difference is that you are helping other people accept their response without judgement. Here are some examples of ways to do so:

- 'I can see that you are really under the pump with that deadline. With all that going on, it is easy to get overwhelmed and feel stressed. How are you feeling?' 'What strategies do you have in place to handle things?'

- 'Of course you are anxious. It is totally normal to feel like that before a big exam. I always get anxious before an exam.'

- 'I completely understand. If I were in your situation, I would have done the same thing.'

- 'I think most people would have felt the same way you did.'

- 'You are upset about getting picked last for sport. I understand why you would be so upset. I used to hate it when I was at school and kids picked me last. It made me feel so sad.'

Responding with empathy helps build trust, connection and engagement with the person going through the struggle. Once these have been established, you have a strong platform from which to support that person into embracing struggle. Like we talked about in the previous chapter, the other benefit of validating how people feel and accepting their reaction, is that it helps them move on from the struggle quicker and into constructive action. These types of responses also really help children understand and deal with their emotions. Say you are in a shop and you are having to line up for ages to get served. When your four year old decides to have a melt down. Normally in that situation we tell them to stop and that it's not okay to do that. Which we all know will not work. A far better approach is to get down on their level and say, 'It can be really hard to wait your turn. I sometimes feel angry and frustrated when I have to wait. I want to yell and stamp my feet and tell people to hurry up. Do you want to play a game to make it more fun?'. This approach, of acknowledging their feelings and telling them that it's okay to feel that way and other people feel that too, helps to move the child more quickly into a constructive space.

What you don't want to say are things like:

- 'Come on, it's not that bad, stop blowing it out of proportion.'

- 'Stop crying, you shouldn't get upset. I will buy you an ice-cream.'

- 'You are overreacting. It's not that bad.'

- 'Don't worry, it's nothing.'

- 'That is a ridiculous thought, stop saying that.'

In chapter 1, I talk about the devastating impact not validating a person's feelings has on privileged people who are shut down by others when they express unhappiness. When we are judged by others for our response to challenge, we heap guilt and shame on top of the difficulty we are already experiencing.

I use this strategy with my children every day. When they behaved badly I used to go into battle against them and it always made the situation worse. Now I lead with validation and acceptance for their thoughts and feelings. Recently my eldest daughter had a friend over and my youngest was trying to play with them. After a while they got tired of having a 6 year old hanging around and were excluding her. I asked my youngest to put her plate away and she yelled and screamed at me and walked off. I just went into her room and said 'Are you feeling left out and alone?', she said 'yes'. I replied 'I used to hate it when people left me out of games. I used to feel angry and sad at the same time. How do you feel?' We chatted some more, she told me how she felt and then she said 'I am sorry for yelling at you Daddy' and gave me a hug. It was a 3 minute conversation that turned her around and got a great result. I said 'How about you and I go play a game instead?' Compare that to me ranting and raving at her, it would have made everything worse.

My kids still have clear boundaries and consequences for poor behaviour. However validating their thoughts and feelings solves many situations so much faster and has dramatically lessened the conflict in our home.

I shared this with a group in a workshop and a women came up and said 'Every day my son says he doesn't want to go to school and has huge tantrums where he gets very angry and anxious. Listening to you I realise that I say things to him like "Change your attitude, focus on the great things about school, look at the positives"'. I said, 'Here is what I want you to do. Go home and when he says those things validate him. Say things like 'I know how you feel. Some days I don't want to go to work. I think I would rather stay at home and watch TV. It can be so hard to do things you don't want to do. What is it about school you don't like?' We spent some time workshopping it. A week later I got this email from her. 'After we spoke last week, I went home and implemented the things we talked about. It has had a huge impact. He is still saying he doesn't want to go to school but there is no longer the intense emotion and sadness behind his words. They are almost just words which is a big change for him! I cannot thank you enough for what you have opened my eyes to throughout this course. I will be forever grateful for the knowledge and skills you have shared with me.'

Connect the struggle to their purpose

Focus their mind on their driving purpose, and remind them of how the struggle gets them closer to their purpose—whether that purpose is related to a goal they want to achieve, a level of mastery they want to obtain or some sort of contribution to others. Doing this allows you to not only help people strive and overcome struggle but also understand them on a deeper level.

As an example of this, we run an online program that focuses on building culture within teams. One of the activities in this program is getting each member of the team to articulate where they find meaning and purpose in their role. After this activity, one leader said, 'Having that conversation gave me huge insight into my team. I am starting to understand them better and because of that I feel more connected to them'. Also, when they run into setback and struggle I relate it back to their meaning and purpose and why they would want to push through that challenge.

Use previous examples

When the person is struggling, outline times when they have overcome similar challenges. Also point out how proud of themselves they were when they overcame that challenge and didn't give up. You can say to them, for example,

- 'It's so frantic right now coming up to year end, and I know that target is a huge challenge, but I have seen you pull it out of the bag before.'

- 'I know you are freaking out about the presentation you have to give to the leaders, and it is totally normal to feel like that before a big presentation. What I have noticed is that the presentations you do best are the ones you feel most nervous about.'

- 'I know you have to have a hard conversation with a member of your team. Those things suck. I always get nervous beforehand, and I am sure you are too. One thing I have noticed about you is that you have an amazing ability to stay composed in the moment and say the right thing and not let your emotions take over.'

Where possible, also share examples of when you have been in a similar situation and have embraced the struggle they are facing. The key focus here is to point out to people specific behaviours that you have seen them use in the past to become successful.

Highlight character traits

Describe the positive traits they are displaying, such as being tenacious, brave, vulnerable or compassionate. This helps people who are in struggle to focus on the constructive behaviours needed. You can say, for example, 'I know this is really challenging for you but what I see is that you are digging deep and being really tenacious. Despite the setbacks and roadblocks, you are not giving up.'

Explore possible strategies

Outline some of the strategies you see them using to solve their challenges.

For example:

- 'How you collaborated with the team to access additional resources and get their insights was genius. I saw how much time it saved you. It was such a great idea.'

- 'I could hear that that customer was being really difficult and demanding, and that must have been really frustrating. It was awesome how you were constantly empathic with them and you kept asking them what outcome they wanted. It was such a great strategy to involve them in the solution and to get them to take ownership.'

Focus on growth achieved

Lastly, focus on the knowledge gained and insights they have developed from their time in struggle. This taps into the progress principle and how when we see ourselves making progress we are more tenacious and better able to handle struggle.

For example, 'I know this has been a hard project to get across the line. However, I see how much more confident you are in front of clients, and your knowledge of that industry has really skyrocketed'.

Improving psychological safety

In 2012, Google embarked on an internal research project code-named 'Project Aristotle'. The focus of this project was to study teams within Google to understand what factors created the ultimate team. This project uncovered five key factors that drove high performance in teams, with the most important being psychological safety. (If you're worried about not being able to sleep after reading this and not knowing the other four, they are dependability (completing things on time), structure and clarity (having clear goals and roles), meaning (the work is important), and impact (thinking the work makes an impact).)

Google defined psychological safety as team members feeling safe to take risks and be vulnerable in front of each other. In other words, that feeling of, 'My team has my back and they are a soft place to land if I screw up'. Since this research was published, the interest in psychological safety has exploded and everyone is talking about it.

In my team's research, we also found that safety plays a huge role in striving—that is, 'Do I feel safe to strive? If I take on something new or challenging, will the people around me support me? Also, do I feel safe to talk about my struggle, and that I won't be judged or blamed or shamed for admitting I am struggling?'

Our research showed that the following dramatically increased safety in a team situation.

Our reactions to people being vulnerable

The definition of vulnerability varies; however, I see vulnerability as putting yourself out there even when you can't guarantee the outcome.

Vulnerability exists in multiple forms, such as:

- asking a question in a meeting
- putting forward an idea you have in a public forum
- asking for feedback on your leadership
- admitting you are wrong
- having a hard conversation with someone
- telling your partner that you are not happy in the relationship

- speaking up when a friend does a behaviour that is anti-social, sexist or racist

- speaking up when people at work behave unethically.

How we treat people when they are vulnerable directly affects their perception of safety. For example, if a child shares something deeply personal and vulnerable with their parents and the parents freak out, get mad, judge them or rant and rave, that child will no longer feel safe with them and the chance of the child stepping into vulnerability again will be extremely low.

Our reactions to people screwing up

When people take on challenge and it doesn't work out, the reaction of the people around them has a huge impact on that individual and affects whether they will embrace struggle into the future. When people fail in the face of struggle, all they want is empathy and understanding.

How about this idea? When someone fails in your life, treat them like you're on the same football team. (Hear me out—I am going somewhere with this.) When a football player makes a mistake on the field, what do the rest of the team do? They run in and make physical contact. They will tap them on the head or pat them on the back. Why the physical touch? Because the person who made the mistake is obviously feeling terrible and the team's behaviour of touch tells them, 'It is okay, we still have your back, let's move on'.

They don't walk up to the player and say something like, 'Are you serious? We could have scored then if you didn't drop the ball'. The player does not need to be told that they just screwed up—they know! Or the other players don't start coaching them on how to do it differently: 'Next time, here is what you need to do'. Or they don't run over to the side of the field and say, 'Hey coach, that wasn't me that was him. I had nothing to do with that. I know I was close to him but I had nothing to do with it'. They don't shame them or coach them or hang them out to dry. They display empathy ('That must suck, that must hurt to fail like that') and acceptance ('It's okay, you are still part of the team').

So when people screw up and fail, don't pretend like it didn't happen. Instead, show them compassion, empathy and acceptance. That response is what helps them move on faster and allows them to perform better. You can discuss the details and what they could do differently down the track, but don't do that in the moment of failure.

> **When people screw up and fail, don't pretend like it didn't happen. Instead, show them compassion, empathy and acceptance.**

I talk to people every day who say they don't feel safe admitting to a mistake because it will be held against them. In this sort of environment, we cover up our mistakes or seek to blame them on others.

Talking about failure without associating shame to it

Working with hundreds and hundreds of teams over the years, one thing has become apparent to me. Most teams and organisations have a dysfunctional relationship with failure. If they actually talk about failure (which is rare), they normally move rapidly to blame. Rather than learning from the failure, they just look for a place to unload it.

One of the most interesting interactions I have ever had was with a major car manufacturer. I spent two weeks at their plant doing some consulting work. Shortly after my arrival, the factory manager was giving me a guided tour. At one point we walked past a large area that had yellow tape on the ground as a boundary and in the centre was a bunch of random car parts. I asked him what it was and he told me it was their screw up pile. I replied, 'Your what?!'

He said, 'They are all the mistakes we have made. At the end of the week, we get together and work out what we need to do with our mistakes'. I knew I had to attend that meeting and, when it rolled around, it was one of the most fascinating things I had ever seen.

All the factory workers stood around the square and a guy with a clip board walked up to the first car part and said, 'Whose is this?' A group would put their hand up and he would then ask them a series of questions about what happened, what caused it and what are they going to do next. Replies ranged from, 'We know exactly what happened and we are in the process of fixing it' to, 'We have no idea and we are still trying to sort it out'. What was most interesting was people took rapid ownership of mistakes and any air of fear or blame was completely absent. None of the groups argued about who the mistake belonged to, and there was no finger pointing. As a result, they sorted the problem rapidly and moved forward.

To create a safe environment, we have to talk about failure in a functional way.

Showing people we care about them

Do we truly care about people or treat them like a commodity? Do we see them as something that just churns out work or do we have a deep and strong connection with them? A key step to making people feel safe at work is showing them you care about them.

CARE AND SAFETY

I was running a project with the safety team of a large petroleum company. Members of this team went out to different workplaces and did safety audits to ensure that the workers at those locations were compliant and following safe working practices. Considering their role, you can probably guess how popular these people were when they entered workplaces. That's right; they are not liked at all. The workers saw them as the safety police, there to get them in trouble. However, there was one stand out.

A young guy (about 29) was loved by the teams he visited. They rated him highly and even invited him to their Christmas party. One of the sites he looked after was a major airport and he was responsible for the workers who refuelled the planes. I asked him how he achieved this amazing result. He said,

I see my role as being part of their team. I am there to help them be safer. I am not there to catch them out or use a big stick on them. The key thing is to show the team that I genuinely care about their wellbeing.

Asked for an example, he said,

Second day on the job, it is 42 °. I walk out on the tarmac and it has to be 60 ° plus. It was brutal. I thought, *Stuff the safety audit. My job is to help these guys to not get heat stroke.* I went back inside and bought a bunch of ice blocks and water bottles. I then went around and gave them to the team. Then I went and found a bunch of towels, wet them and put them in the freezer. I spent the whole day bringing each of the guys cold towels and keeping them hydrated to help them deal with the heat. From that day on, they loved me. Every guy in that team knows I genuinely give a shit about them. That was the start and it just got better from there.

SUMMARY

- Supporting others to strive and overcome struggle not only helps them grow and evolve but also builds an incredibly strong bond.

- Help people strive through the following:

  - Stop rescuing people; instead, when appropriate, let them sit with the discomfort that is inherent in the strive.

  - Show people empathy and validate their response to struggle. Don't judge their reaction, but instead accept it.

  - Help them connect the strive to their meaning and purpose.

  - Remind them of previous examples where they overcame struggle and discomfort.

  - Highlight the character traits they are displaying, such as courage, tenacity, creativity and bravery.

  - Point out the specific strategies they are using to strive, such as collaboration or systems thinking.

  - Focus on and celebrate with them the growth they have achieved from striving.

- A critical step in helping people strive is to build psychological safety in their environment. You can do this by:

  - responding constructively when they exhibit vulnerability

  - supporting them when they screw up

  - openly discussing failure without attaching guilt and shame to it

  - showing you care about them.

Conclusion

So, there you have it: ten years of research boiled down into one book. Now for this conclusion, I must summarise the message of the book into one or two punchy yet somewhat pithy pages. Hmmm, no pressure. Here we go!

People today have totally bought into the misconception that negative thoughts and emotions are bad and bad for us, and positive emotions and thoughts are good and good for us. As a result, we go to great lengths to avoid uncomfortable states such as uncertainty, anxiety, confusion and fear. Instead, we are drawn to comfort, happiness and certainty like moths to a flame. However, the avoidance of uncomfortable states leads to a wasted life or a life that is half-baked. This reduces our fulfilment and self-esteem, and ultimately has a detrimental impact on our wellbeing and mental health. How can I be so convinced of this? Thousands of research participants told us so. Here are the key points we have learned.

1. *Human beings are most fulfilled when striving towards a meaningful goal, vision or aspiration:* The striving is not about arriving at the end goal but getting in the trenches with the struggle that is inherent in all striving.

2. *The most gratifying striving involves the greatest level of struggle:* We get cuts and bruises, and sometimes struggle gets the best of us, but if we don't retreat, we crawl out of the trenches a better and more evolved version of ourselves. The courage and evolution that occurs in the strive is what we crave. They are the elements that lead to the greatest level of fulfilment. However, society has been sold on this lie that the best life is an easy and pleasurable one. As a result, we seek comfort and happiness. This attitude makes us waste the strive because we are so obsessed with getting the result or staying comfortable that we miss the gold and learnings in the strive.

3. *To effectively handle struggle, we need to view it as the pathway to development:* We cannot evolve without experiencing discomfort. When we have this mindset, we are able to sit with the discomfort long enough to evolve. In contrast, too many people see struggle as a threat and, therefore, they retreat back to old safe and comfortable behaviours that make them feel good in the moment but do not allow evolution to happen.

4. *The way to see struggle as development is, when faced with it, accept your reaction to the struggle (positive or negative) without judgement:* Instead, focus on the meaning and purpose on the other side of the struggle and marvel at your own courage.

5. *In order to strive more in your life, implement rituals to build a strong platform from which you can strive:* These rituals are honing your mental focus, being grateful, practising recovery, celebrating victory and connecting deeply with others.

The complete model sums up these points perfectly.

The preceding points are what I have learned from the more than 100000 data points we have collected in the past ten years and countless hours of analysis. In fact, I have spent so many hours staring at a screen, I now wear glasses. True story.

But I want to finish this book in more of a 'human mode', with less reliance on numbers and data.

I believe everyone has a super power. Some people can come up with marvellous inventions, some people can create amazing works of art, and others can hug with the appropriate amount of pressure for the right length of time. My super power is that people feel safe to confide in me. For some unknown reason, they feel secure to take off the mask and tell me what is really going on.

Because of the type of work I do on a daily basis, I find myself having these deep conversations often. Here is what these vulnerable souls tell me. Most people are scared. Scared of losing their job, scared of being alone, scared of being a terrible parent, scared of screwing up, scared of not being enough and scared of being found out as a fraud. The fallout of this fear is we let it rule our lives, we hold back, we play small or we overcompensate by being overly competitive and aggressive. We let those stories inside our head run our lives and bully us. But we are tired of being scared. We want fulfilment and to display courage so badly it is literally oozing out of the pores of our skin.

I encourage you to engage in striving more, to stop being attached to the result but rather soak up the strive and all the gifts it has to offer. See the struggle as an opportunity to develop by accepting that it is going to be difficult and scary, marvelling at your courage and connecting to the meaning and purpose that sits on the other side. Finally, I implore you to get in the trenches and fight it out with the things that scare the hell out of you and, most of all, fall in love with the work.

Index

Printed and bound by CPI Group (UK) Ltd, Croydon, CR0 4YY

17/07/2024

14529268-0001